GRANT—
TAKE IT TO THE BANK!

WHAT READERS ARE SAYING ABOUT *WHY THEY BUY*

"The ability to sell is the number one skill in business. You've got to sell! Cheri Tree will teach you how."

— Robert Kiyosaki, Founder of the Rich Dad Company and Cashflow Technologies, Inc. and Author of the *Rich Dad Poor Dad* series

"B.A.N.K. is a game changer for every entrepreneur and sales professional. This system will strengthen your confidence, expand your selling skills, and dramatically increase your income."

— Les Brown, World-Renowned Motivational Coach, Speaker, and Best-Selling Author

"B.A.N.K. is a scientifically validated system designed to convert psychology into buyology—the science of buying behavior."

— Dr. Ryan T. Howell, Associate Professor of Psychology, San Francisco State University, and Co-Founder of Beyond The Purchase

"This book guides you through the process of what so many have attempted to do and only a few have achieved—the mastery of closing the sale. Don't just read this book; study it and master it!"

— Sandra Yancey, CEO and Founder, eWomenNetwork, Inc.

"As a psychologist, I can tell you it is imperative for salespeople to know the personality traits, decision-making models, and personalities of the people they are selling to. Cheri Tree's B.A.N.K. codes does that for you so simply you will not need a psychologist to go on sales appointments with you! Learn the secret individual buying codes and you'll have more customers than you'll know what to do with!"

— Laura Herring, Psychologist, Author of *No Fear Allowed* and Founder and Chair Emeritus of IMPACT Group

"Through her book, *Why They Buy*, Cheri Tree delivers the magic and missing link to better understand and connect with others from their perspectives. The concepts and tools masterfully captured in this book have shape-shifted the way I personally relate to others and has exponentially accelerated our business growth over the past seven years."

— Jenny Luetkemeyer, Co-Founder and EVP of Global Operations, BANKCODE

"This book is a remarkable, new, and simple approach for closing sales that will definitely increase your income!"

— Barbara Corcoran, Investor on *Shark Tank*

"Cheri Tree may very well be the most brilliant business mind in the world today! Her BANKCODE sales training is the absolute best I have ever experienced in my thirty-five years in sales. It is easy to understand and even easier to apply to all your complex prospects currently in your sales funnel. If you want to grow your income by as much as ten times, invest in yourself by applying BANKCODE's sales training to your life and business. It may become the single greatest business investment you ever make!"

— Patrick Snow, Professional Keynote Speaker, Publishing Coach, and International Best-Selling Author of *Creating Your Own Destiny*

"Your business depends on sales. How you see people and how people see you will determine whether your client will buy or walk away. B.A.N.K. will reveal to you how to improve your chances of closing the deal, whether it's in business, relationships, or even your own life. Having met the team behind the B.A.N.K. CODE, I know this book will help you elevate your business and life to a much higher level. Read it, study it, and take your profits to the bank."

— Sandy Jadeja, Chief Market Strategist, Signal Pro

"Cheri Tree is a force of nature. Her authentic passion and caring touches everyone. Her insights into buying behavior and her message could not be more powerful."

— Joyce Brown, Founder, The Sales Savvy CEO

"This book opened my eyes to the powerful idea of simplifying the sales conversation. Cheri Tree's genius is observing the buying behavior and distilling it down to a simple system."

— LeAnn Pashina, President, Creatively Communicate, Inc.

"Cheri Tree is one of those entrepreneurs who has discovered the secret, the science, and the system of cracking someone's buying behavior in less than ninety seconds.

She's an inspiration and always entertaining. You owe it to yourself to read this book."

— Dawn Moore, Professional Development Strategist, Rapport Management Group, LLC

"*Why They Buy* is far and away the most useful, simple approach to the sales process I've ever seen. The content is bulletproof. You have to read this book."

— Julie Stephens, Partner, The Sales Savvy CEO

"*Why They Buy* teaches you how to connect instead of contact, and how to serve instead of sell. It will unlock the secrets of how to connect the brain, heart, and wallet, and as a result, improve communication, strengthen key relationships, and increase sales."

— Robert Bloom, CEO, Aquipa Partners, Sweden

"I've known Cheri for years and have worked as a performance psychologist for decades. This book is a game-changer and accelerates your selling/closing connectivity with others—you need to read and live this code because it is a trajectory changer!"

— Dr. Jeffrey Magee, CMC, CBE, PDM, CSP, Human Capital Developer, Best-Selling Author, and Publisher of *Performance/P360 Magazine*

"The methodology in this book has changed my life! I'm now able to deliver my presentation and communication style the right way 100 percent of the time. This book is a must for any business owner and his or her team. *Why They Buy* provides a powerful, practical, and simple system for running your business."

— Brigitta Hoeferle, Founder, Owner, and Principal of the Montessori School of Cleveland

"Cheri Tree has found a way to touch the business heart of every man and woman. This book shares her authentic extraordinary stories, offering you a look into her life and how she created this life-changing methodology."

— Esther Wildenberg, Co-Founder and EVP of Global Sales, BANKCODE

"This practical, enjoyable book shows you how to increase your sales and income faster than you ever thought possible."

— Brian Tracy, Author of *The Psychology of Selling*

"As a veterinarian and practice owner for over twenty years, I encountered several personality systems. That is why I *instantly* recognized BANK as a quantum leap beyond the others for harmonious client and staff interactions and smooth, productive operations. B.A.N.K.'s genius and power is in its simplicity. IT WORKS!"

— Marilyn Millman, DVM

"Through the lens of her sales and entrepreneurial journey, with all of its ups and downs, Cheri Tree has written with honesty and passion. This book is not just recommended reading; it's required."

— Linda Cousineau, CEO, LPC and Associates, Inc.

"What a twist! Understanding why people buy vs. the same old sales tricks will revolutionize your business. I have been using Cheri's teachings for years and made millions. Thanks, Cheri!"

— Joshua Higginbotham, Top Producing Sales and Marketing Specialist, Author and Trainer

"To master your business, you have to master sales. The living master and teacher of sales and how to make your business a masterpiece is Cheri Tree. Reading this book will change your life."

— Leon Tarasoff, President, Active Play Toys and Games, Inc.

"Cheri's description of visiting the candy factory with her grandfather as a teenager made me realize how truly profound Cheri's approach to sales communication development is. Although there are many psychologists who develop personality and communication style inventories, Cheri approaches sales success from a much deeper, more personal perspective. B.A.N.K. is not theory. It comes from decades of real world, person-to-person direct sales experience. Cheri's commitment to understanding people's needs is BANK."

— Professor Mark Darius Juszczak, St. John's University, Department of Mass Communication

"This book is a remarkably new and simple approach for closing sales that will drastically increase your income."

— Sher Murata, Regional Manager, KSRR Landscape Management Inc.

"The B.A.N.K. system is a game-changer for anyone serious about creating more success in any industry. The priceless process you will learn will allow you to connect with prospects instantly and close more deals. I have personally watched Cheri introduce this program to leaders all over the world, and the results have been magnificent!"

— Bill Walsh, Business Coach and Best-Selling Author

"This book has taken my closing skills to an all-time high. It's a must read for any salesperson, entrepreneur, business owner, and professional."

— Stephanie Bonte-Lebair, Founder, The Empowered Voice

"This is the most powerful, persuasive, inspiring, and practical book on becoming the best salesperson that you will ever read. It's loaded with ideas, insights, true stories, and formulas that will change the way you communicate and close the sale. Cheri Tree is a genius! I've learned a lot from her and you will too!"

— Mark Bertrand, Entrepreneur and Former Teaching Assistant at Harvard University for the Master's Course "Entrepreneurship: Launching an E-Commerce Startup."

"The bottom line is that Cheri Tree is number one in the world at what she does, and you can take that to the bank!"

— Brad Lea, CEO, Lightspeed VT

"The most important book ever written on the subject of closing the sale."

— Jennifer Draper, Owner, The Draper Group

"*Why They Buy* is absolutely the right book for our times—inspiring, empowering, and immediately useful. My greatest wonder is why it wasn't written before! It identifies the missing link in the sales process and closes the gap for increased profitability and success."

— Hyrum Smith, Co-Founder of Franklin Covey Co.

"The B.A.N.K. system is a powerful moneymaker. It just helped me close a $2.5 million deal in record time. B.A.N.K. helps me consistently reach more people more effectively.

But B.A.N.K. has also dramatically improved my relationship with my wife! Thank you, Cheri Tree and team!

— Brett Yeager, Sales Strategist, Brett Yeager and Associates

"I learned more from reading this book than in the past twenty years in business! *Why They Buy* is a game-changer for every business owner, entrepreneur, and corporate executive."

— Mark Shuler, President, The Shuler Group

"*Why They Buy* is the first book I literally could not put down. Read this book and watch all of your significant relationships transform."

— Jaime Edgar Taets, CEO and Co-Founder, Keystone Strategy Group

"In this life-changing book, you'll learn how to increase your income dramatically. By using this proven system, Cheri Tree went from zero to millionaire in less than three years."

— Sandy Hayakawa, Founder and CEO, House of H. Properties, LLC

"Excellent stories with simple techniques! This book abolishes the question of "Why They Buy."

— Adam Markel, International Speaker, Attorney, CEO, and #1 *Wall Street Journal* Best-Selling Author of *Soul Over Matter* and *Pivot: The Art & Science of Reinventing Your Career and Life*

"Cheri Tree is electrifying! She has the ability to transfix readers, motivate them, empower them, and give them great information in a way they can absorb fully. I've seen a lot of speakers, trainers, and authors, but none are as authentic, charismatic, and dynamic as Cheri Tree."

**— Dawn Shuler, CEO and Founder,
The Shuler Group, LLC**

"This is the most powerful, persuasive, inspiring, and practical book you will ever read on becoming the best salesperson. It's loaded with ideas, insights, true stories, and formulas that will change the way you communicate and close the sale. Cheri Tree is a genius! I've learned a lot from her and you will too."

— Shelly Pereira, President, Verance Consulting

"Cheri Tree has dissected the metrics of communication and behavior, and developed a masterful system of efficient communication to propel sales. She is a force of nature, and her product is a major contribution to science and society."

**— Dr. Hans S. Keirstead, Chairman and
CEO of AIVITA Biomedical**

"I could not put this book down. It's exactly what business leaders need today. Cheri discusses with clarity and insight how people make their buying decisions. Everyone should make time to read this book."

**— Adam Majrouh, Founder and CEO,
Grow Empower Inspire**

"This is a powerful read—brave, intelligent, imaginative, amazingly prescient, and backed up by a proven system and methodology. A must-read book for anyone in any form of sales and communication."

— Raquel M. Tillman, President, The Sales Rhino

"B.A.N.K. is able to distill the essence of selling and influence to a science. It is a fast and highly effective system that teaches you to speak the language of your prospects, build nurturing relationships, and accelerate buying decisions."

— James Leong C. Foo, Adjunct Professor, National University of Singapore, Master Trainer, Visions.One Consulting Pte Ltd.

"In *Why They Buy*, Cheri Tree reveals the formula for how to crack someone's buying behavior in less than ninety seconds. This book is revolutionary."

— Garth Farrant, Managing Director, Personal Development South Africa

WHY THEY BUY

CRACKING THE PERSONALITY CODE TO ACHIEVE RECORD SALES AND REAL WEALTH

CHERI TREE
FOUNDER & CEO | BANKCODE

WHY THEY BUY
Cracking the Personality Code to Achieve Record Sales and Real Wealth

Published by:
Aviva Publishing
Lake Placid, NY
(518) 523-1320
www.AvivaPubs.com

Cheri Tree
Telephone: (702) 342-0742
Email: whytheybuy@bankcode.com
Web: WhyTheyBuy.com | CheriTree.com | BANKCODE.com

ISBN: 978-1-944335-68-7
Library of Congress Control Number: 2017904745

Editor: Tyler Tichelaar, Superior Book Productions
Cover Designer: Svetlana Hodoba
Interior Layout & Design: Fusion Creative Works, fusioncw.com
Presentation Designer: Cory Jim, Empowered Presentations
Author Photo: Walter Johnson

Every attempt has been made to source all quotes properly.

Printed in the United States of America

First Edition
2 4 6 8 10 12

“Any fool can complicate things; it takes a genius to simplify them.”

— Albert Einstein

DEDICATION

To my beautiful wife and business partner, Esther Wildenberg, for your unconditional love, support, and encouragement to share my gifts with the world. You are the most amazing entrepreneur and business partner in the world! You are my angel, and I'm so grateful to you for sharing your light with me so I can serve others. Getting a Yes from you was the best Yes of my life!

To my best friend and business partner, Jenny Luetkemeyer, for your unshakeable loyalty and standing by my side, even in the face of extreme adversity, and for helping me see that B.A.N.K. was the message I needed to share with the world.

To my mom, Sallianne Tree, who believed in me my entire life, programmed me to believe that anything was possible, and taught me to shoot for the moon. And to my dad, Norm Tree, who celebrated my wins and encouraged me never to quit during the tough times by having me join him with positive affirmations of, "Yes! Yes! Yes!"

To my brother, Tom, who always believed in me from the very beginning. I look forward to building this company with you! Remember, it's what we dream that sets us apart.

To my entire family for supporting and believing in me during the ups and, more importantly, during the downs.

To Chad Wade and Justin Yates, who died way too early in a tragic plane crash. You taught me so much about teamwork and leadership. I loved being in the million-dollar club with you and traveling the world. You are still making a difference in millions of lives, including mine. You may be gone, but never forgotten.

To all my mentors, leaders, and guides who have coached, taught, trained, led, and guided me to greatness. Your books, seminars, classes, workshops, boot camps, mentoring, and masterminding with me have been priceless. Thank you for sharing your wisdom with me so I would be ready to share mine with the world.

To the most incredible team that works with my company, BANKCODE. Your support, encouragement, faith in me, loyalty, hard work, dedication, and commitment to sharing our message with the world has been the fuel I've needed to forge ahead, take risks, make tough decisions, overcome the obstacles, and build a company that puts people before profits and is committed to making a difference, not just a dollar.

To every member of our global community, B.A.N.K. Nation. Our clients, our consultants, and our beloved B.A.N.K.

Trainers. You are the wind beneath my wings! Your success stories inspire me to work harder, build faster, and push stronger as we unite around the world to bring our collective vision of *B.A.N.K., the language of people*, and to manifest our vision, "ONE WORLD, ONE LANGUAGE," to every family, every community, and eventually, all of humanity.

And last but not least, I dedicate this book to every entrepreneur who has ever had the courage to start a business and failed. To every salesperson who has attempted to close a sale only to be slammed with rejection and the inevitable "No." To every network marketer who has recruited a new distributor only to have him or her quit a few months later. To every company that has struggled to hire the right team members. To every insurance agent who has had a chargeback. To every real estate professional who's ever lost a listing. To every attorney who has lost a trial. To every doctor who attempts to communicate with a patient, or his or her family. To every business owner who has lost a deal and been edged out by a competitor. To every person or student who's ever been bullied. To every employee who's ever been denied a raise or a promotion. To every leader who has failed to duplicate himself or herself and is exhausted going full speed. To every lover who has ever lost a relationship. To every parent who has ever had a breakdown in communication with his or her children, or had a teenager vow to run away. Ultimately, I dedicate this book to you, the reader. May you crack the code to your life's Holy Grail and learn how to unlock the secrets, the science, and the system to getting more yeses, regardless of your occupation or vocation.

CONTENTS

"Here's to the crazy ones, the misfits, the rebels, the troublemakers, the round pegs in the square holes...the ones who see things differently—they're not fond of rules. You can quote them, disagree with them, glorify or vilify them, but the only thing you can't do is ignore them because they change things...they push the human race forward, and while some may see them as the crazy ones, we see genius, because the ones who are crazy enough to think that they can change the world, are the ones who do."

— Steve Jobs

INTRODUCTION
FINDING A BETTER WAY

Which of these three statements best describes you?

1. YOU SUCK AT SALES! You're scared of rejection. You avoid selling like the plague. You deny the fact that you're even in sales. You're chasing your tail, filling your pipeline with suspects instead of prospects. You're caught in a vicious trap and you're losing the *numbers game*. Your income is down. Your job is on the line or you may even need to close your business. You're one "No" away from throwing in the towel and abandoning your life in sales as a business owner or entrepreneur. Your dreams are turning into vapor and you're losing hope that you'll ever make it big.

2. YOU CRUSH IT IN SALES! You're the lucky one—the top 5 percent! You've been told that you can sell ice to Eskimos and stripes to a tiger! You're the top producer in your company and the envy of every other salesperson on the team! Your name is etched on nearly every plaque on your company's wall of fame! You are the golden child in your organization and claim to have the Midas Touch, closing nearly every sale that comes your way. You wake up feeling alive and can't wait to dial for dollars, knowing you're that much closer to winning the big contest and earning your next bonus check! Somehow you have cracked the code—and yet you have no idea how you actually do it. (If this is you, hang in there because I'm going to reveal the code you've cracked so you can keep cracking it and help others on your team to do the same.)

3. YOU'RE A COMPANY EXECUTIVE RUNNING THE SALES ORGANIZATION. You're trying to solve the puzzle as to why the top 20 percent of your sales team does 80 percent of the sales volume, and the remaining 80 percent can't even seem to hit their quotas. You've invested countless hours and dollars into sales training, but the investment has yielded marginal results. You can't seem to duplicate your top performers and you're frustrated trying to figure out how to create record growth for your company while building a lasting legacy with the organization.

Depending upon which statement you chose, you're either frustrated with some aspect of your business and you're looking for a solution, or you're looking for answers that explain why selling is the easiest thing you've ever done and why others just don't seem to get it.

No matter where you are, I can relate because I've experienced all three of the above! I started off at the bottom... the very bottom! My dream of being a successful entrepreneur got crushed when I realized that I sucked at sales. I was so terrible that during my entire first year in sales as a commission-only part-time financial advisor I only earned $700. I was the worst salesperson on the team! For five years, I studied every sales training program I could get my hands on. I read dozens of books, listened to audios, watched webinars, attended seminars...all to no avail. I even hired coaches and mentors and paid them thousands of dollars (money I didn't have), and still, nothing was making a significant difference. I felt like throwing in the towel and giving up, but I was too stubborn to quit!

Then suddenly, the game changed. I discovered a missing link in the sales process and cracked the code to making millions and millions of dollars. The next thing I knew, I was winning trips, achieving record sales, earning an incredible income, and being featured on magazine covers! I went from zero to hero overnight—and everyone wanted to know my secret.

Here's the question I needed to answer: Was I the exception, or did I discover something that could be taught, transferred, and duplicated to other salespeople, and scaled across an entire organization? When most top producers get asked how they do it, they typically don't have a clear answer—they just know that they do it! This lack of an answer is frustrating to everyone else on the team, including company executives who are trying to figure out how to clone their top people. Luckily, I discovered something that could, in fact, be taught, transferred, and duplicated to others—and that's why I wrote this book!

In this book, you will learn the greatest secret in the world—*why they buy*. I will unlock the secrets, the science, and the system you need to supercharge your sales in less than ninety seconds! You will discover why you have been trapped and struggling with the sales game and learn how to win the game. You will uncover the science behind the sales process and learn how to avoid making the most common mistakes salespeople unknowingly make—costing fortunes in lost revenue. You will learn the system you need to master to close more sales and earn more money than ever before—allowing you to create real wealth and an even greater quality of life!

I challenge you to read this book cover to cover and apply the wisdom I have learned over the past twenty years, following the step-by-step strategies and techniques I will teach you in each section. When you do, you will find yourself on the fast track to record sales and accumulating real wealth that you can *take to the bank*!

As a result of following this exact system, I was able to take my annual income from $72,000 to over $1 million within three years. I hit sales records that have never been hit before—and have never been broken since—when I took my income from $8,000 per month to more than $261,000 per month in twenty-eight days! The B.A.N.K. system supercharged my sales in a way that made me feel like I was a superhero, and the rest, they say, is history!

My discovery landed me on stage at some of the biggest business conferences in the world, sharing my strategies with tens of thousands of sales professionals, business owners, and entrepreneurs. I've had the honor to share the stage with Tony Robbins, Robert Kiyosaki, Les Brown, Suze Orman, and Sir Richard Branson. I was invited to speak and lecture at Harvard University and the University of California at Berkeley. I've been nominated as Entrepreneur of the Year and Innovator of the Year by various organizations and associations. I've even had my work undergo significant scientific review by San Francisco State University, which published a white paper indicating that my system could predict buying behavior in less than ninety seconds and that anyone who used this methodology would likely experience an increase in sales. Even with all of this success, I still find myself on a journey of discovery, learning new ways to master my craft each and every day. The world is my classroom, and I'm so thankful for all the lessons it teaches me from people like you, not only in sales, but in relationships too.

I understand why you may not have reached all of your goals thus far. You may be working a full-time job and moonlighting as an entrepreneur. You may be a single parent trying to juggle your business and your life. You may be a top producer, but you find yourself working too hard and not having enough free time. You may be buried in your work projects with no time to dedicate to figuring out how to beat the numbers game. You may just simply feel stuck or frozen, not knowing what to do next. I get it. I've been there—just like you!

And that is why I wrote this book—for you! I want to be your mentor, your coach, and your consultant. I want to help you navigate the path to great success. I will guide you along the journey, helping you to avoid costly pitfalls, and show you the blueprint to success. I want to be your go-to person when you're frustrated and ready to give up! I want to be the advisor you can count on to help you prep for every sales call you have, and I want you to take me on each appointment! I want to help you build an empire and an everlasting legacy! I will be here for you—every step of the journey—all the way to the finish line.

The journey of a thousand miles begins with the first step. Are you ready to take that first step? Are you ready to leave failure, frustration, and the status quo in the dust, and live the life you've always imagined? Are you ready to step outside your comfort zone, learn something new, expand your mindset, and become a super-achiever? Are you ready to fast track your company growth and leave your competition in the dust? If so, awesome! Let's get started and take this journey together. Now is your time to achieve big and *take it to the bank!*

"The ability to sell is the number one skill in business. If you cannot sell, don't bother thinking about becoming a business owner."

— Robert Kiyosaki

SECTION 1: THE SECRET

Sales is such an important part of our entire global economy. Robert Kiyosaki declared it the number one skill in business. After all, every single business model in the world depends on sales for sustainable success. They may not be traditional sales, sure. Today, sales can mean many things in many different industries. But at the core of any business is a customer's purchase of your product or service. Your business cannot survive without sales.

The reality is that sales must be maintained; it is the lifeblood of any organization or business. Lack of sales destroys careers, kills businesses, and thwarts dreams. If you aren't closing sales, your business is dying. In fact, a study by Harvard University showed that the only key business priority held by all of the businesses on the Forbes 100 list was sales. No company can be successful without making sales a priority.

Unfortunately, many people struggle with sales. In fact, about three out of four salespeople are essentially ineffective at sales, mostly due to lack of proper training, despite the fact that companies spend millions on sales training every year. In reality, only about 6 percent of salespeople truly excel at their jobs. This means that many organizations are held back from ever reaching their full potential—and many salespeople will never reach the level of success they hope for without the right training.

So what's wrong? Clearly something is missing, some secret to sales that most people seem to miss. If you're like me, you've studied most of the top sales trainings out there, but with only minimal, incremental results. Everyone in the corporate training field claims to have the secret for dramatically improving sales, yet most have fallen short of producing the results people really want.

That's because most people are looking at sales in the wrong way. The system is broken. It's time to start fixing it and approach sales in the right way. It's time to change your mindset and look at sales with a whole new perspective—starting with figuring out *"Why They Buy."*

Why they buy is the critical element every business owner needs to discover and the critical element every salesperson needs to know.

"Why do people buy?" is exponentially more important than "How do I sell?" I'm fascinated that companies will spend thousands of hours and millions of dollars teaching people "how to sell" instead of investing in the only question that ever matters to their bottom line: "Why they buy."

For the last 150 years, salespeople have been taught how to sell. The world is filled with sales gurus, experts, and masters who teach a full spectrum of sales techniques, strategies, closes, methodologies, and systems for selling, yet salespeople continue to fail.

Which is ultimately more important to you: knowing how to sell or knowing why your customer buys? Rather than fruitlessly obsessing over selling, invest your time in learning why people buy everything from products and services to ideas and dreams.

Over the past twenty years, I have been seeking to understand "Why they buy," and I have found some compelling answers, which I'll share in these pages. But first, you need to know four key secrets that can help you understand the truth about sales. I'm going to take you through each one, step-by-step, in this section. These four secrets changed the way I look at sales, allowing me to skyrocket my income and create real wealth—and now you can do the same.

CHAPTER 1

ESCAPING THE SALES MAYTAG

"The distance between insanity and genius is measured only by success."

– Bruce Feirstein

When I was in college, I studied recreation, leadership, and business. I paid my way through school working various part-time jobs and starting a few small businesses. Since I was studying recreation and leadership, I got a job with the university's outdoor recreation program, Outdoors Unlimited. I had the opportunity to become a certified whitewater rafting guide as one of the job perks and help run several rafting trips for the university on the Green River in Southern Utah. It was really fun—and I love to have fun!

Being on the river meant we got to camp, cook, play, party, splash around, and have a great time with our fellow rafters. However, preparing for my certification to become a river guide wasn't all fun and games. On a more sobering note, we had to learn how to survive life and death moments, including escaping the maytag.

MY FIRST MAYTAG

"Maytag" is a term used by river guides to refer to certain places on the river where the water rushes over a large boulder. As the water crashes down in all its fury on the other side, it creates this massive underwater spin cycle known as a maytag. River maytags get their name from the popular washer and dryer brand because they mirror what happens inside a washer. A maytag acts just like a washer in a spin cycle, but on a river, a maytag can kill you.

Maytags are dangerous. The spin cycle beneath the water's surface can be so strong that it can curl you into a spinning ball, keeping you trapped until you run out of oxygen and drown. You are as powerless as clothing in a washer, but unlike your laundry, you won't come out better than you went in.

So just like Harry Houdini, the infamous escape artist from the early twentieth century, escaping a potentially fateful trap, we had to escape the maytag. River guides must be able to save any rafters who accidentally get sucked into a maytag. We had to demonstrate that we could safely get them—and ourselves—out.

On the day of certification, I had to jump into the river feet first, leave my raft behind, and head straight downstream toward the rushing water below to demonstrate I could successfully escape the maytag. I watched a few guides go in front of me until my turn came. Then I jumped into the water with as much courage as I could muster. The closer to the maytag I got, the harder my heart pounded.

I could hear the roar of the water ahead, and I had already passed the point of no return. I kept my feet facing forward and took a huge deep breath as my body got sucked over the boulder and slammed deep into the maytag on the other side.

Just as the name promised, the maytag spun my body in circles underneath the water like a piece of clothing in the washing machine. At this point, I had two choices: panic and follow my instinct to fight the current or follow my training and do just the opposite.

The only way to survive the maytag is to relax your entire body, stretch out all your limbs, let the current push you back to the surface, and continue floating downstream. That's exactly what I did...and it worked!

The training I received as a river guide prepared me to face the maytag, and it saved my life! Once I had conquered the maytag challenge, I felt like I could do anything.

THE SALES MAYTAG

A few years later, after a short time working in corporate America, I decided I was ready for my next challenge...to be an entrepreneur! I had read *Rich Dad, Poor Dad* by Robert Kiyosaki and knew that I wanted to build my own business. With the same courage it took for me to jump into the river, I jumped into sales as a financial advisor—earning commissions only. That was when I encountered another seemingly insurmountable maytag—a *sales maytag.*

Needless to say, I was not an overnight sales success. I was basically the worst salesperson on the entire team. Although every instinct told me I should quit before I drowned, I decided to fight that instinct and keep going. After all, I still thought I was Houdini, and this was the only way I could escape my full-time job and transition to running my own business. I knew there had to be a way to escape the sales maytag.

Over the next five years, I immersed myself in learning everything I could about sales. I read best-selling books. I attended top seminars and boot camps. I listened to popular audio programs. I attended training after training with top experts in the field. I even hired personal sales coaches and paid them hundreds of dollars an hour to teach me their secrets to sales.

During those five years, my sales improved. Within two years, I was able to quit my full-time job, and by the end of the fifth year, I had grown my income to a respectable $72,000 per year. I even won some company bonuses, like awards and trips, thanks to hitting sales targets. But while others were celebrating my success, I still felt like a failure. I had $30,000 in credit card debt (financing all my training programs), was driving a BMW with a salvaged title (so I could "fake it until you make it"), and was renting an apartment for $800 per month. I was trying to qualify to buy my first home, but I was constantly told I couldn't because my income was too low and unpredictable. I felt like I was stuck in the sales maytag, spinning my wheels in sales with no chance of escape.

Then I heard another quote from Kiyosaki. He said,

"Stop taking advice from people more messed up than you!"

– Robert Kiyosaki #WhyTheyBuy

My whole world came crashing down. I felt like the world's biggest hypocrite. Here I was completely in debt with no assets to speak of, and I was a financial advisor trying to tell people what to do with their money.

I was going insane! Something felt broken—and I wasn't sure whether it was me or the system!

ESCAPING THE SALES MAYTAG

The definition of insanity is doing the same thing over and over and expecting different results. Suddenly, I realized

I was living that definition of insanity, completely stuck in my own sales maytag.

It seemed like every sales training I attended kept giving me the same advice, over and over again. Everyone kept telling me that sales was a numbers game, and that in order to get more yeses, I had to get more _________.

Go ahead, fill in the blank! I'm sure you've heard it before. You probably finished the sentence automatically....

"In order to get more yeses, you have to get more nos."

Now, stop and think about this for a moment. To me, this was the craziest thing I'd ever heard—and yet everyone was saying it! This was definitely the definition of insanity! This was the sales maytag everyone was getting sucked into. This meant I had to work longer and harder, chasing the nos so I could try to get more yeses.

Suddenly, I had my "Aha!" moment. I realized it was the system that was broken—not me!

Okay, follow me for a moment. I want you to change the way you've been programmed to think about sales.

In order to get more yeses, you have to get more yeses–not more nos!

@CheriTree #WhyTheyBuy

Doesn't that just make more sense? If this is so obvious, then why is everyone sucked into the numbers game myth and automatically going for no? Because it's a maytag—a sales maytag.

THE REAL COST OF A NO

Getting a no is much more expensive than you think. Let me share with you one of my early experiences with a very expensive no.

I was selling insurance and trying to close the deal with a prospect. The guy wanted to do his due diligence, so a few weeks went by. Finally, I got a call from him one morning telling me that he was ready to sign the contract, so I agreed to meet him for lunch with the paperwork.

Woohoo! I was so excited to get paid! I was about to earn a "comma check," meaning I would earn at least a thousand dollars—money I really needed.

Somehow, in my scramble to get ready for the appointment, I showed up to the restaurant ten minutes late. When I got there, I apologized for being late. Then I proceeded to pull out the paperwork, hand it to him, and get that part of our appointment finished.

Just as I was handing him the paperwork, he put his two hands up to stop me from moving forward. Then he said, "Cheri, wait a minute. Before you go any further, I just want to let you know that I no longer want to do business with you."

I froze in my tracks in total shock. What had I done wrong? He had just called me to say he wanted to sign the contract.

Then, he explained: "Cheri, you were late and you didn't call ahead to tell me you were going to be late. You've disrespected my time. [Ten minutes!] If this is how you treat me before you have my money, imagine how I think I'll be treated once you have it."

Wow! That was a really valuable and expensive lesson. I not only lost thousands of dollars that day, but I lost the lifetime value of my client and his entire referral network.

The cost of that "No" was way more expensive than it originally seemed. I couldn't afford to get sucked into the sales maytag again, so I began documenting every single experience, and the exact reasons that make or break the sale. I desperately needed to crack the code.

I CRACKED THE CODE

The good news is: I cracked the code! I'm going to teach you how to crack the code as well. What I discovered could be one of the greatest breakthroughs in the history of sales.

What if there were a secret I could teach you, a science you could learn, and a system you could follow that would allow you to increase your sales up to 300 percent? What if I could teach you how to escape the sales maytag in less than ninety seconds?

Sound too good to be true? You don't have to read on and get my advice. You can always put the book down and go back to the way you've always been doing sales. No harm, no foul.

But before you do that, let me share my personal story. When I discovered the missing link in sales, I was able to escape the sales maytag and skyrocket my success. Using the B.A.N.K. code, within three years, my annual income surpassed one million dollars—and the rest, they say, is history.

If you're ready to learn how to turn those nos into yeses and earn more money in less time, then I'm going to teach you how to crack the personality code and take it to the bank! All you need to do is read this book and follow the system I developed. I will teach you how to unlock the secrets, the science, and the system to supercharge your sales in less than 90 seconds.

The bottom line is that we've all been taught to do sales wrong. We've been tricked into thinking that sales success is unreachable unless you go through hundreds or even thousands of experiences hearing the most demoralizing word in the world: no. Luckily, that's no longer true. This book is going to show you how to relax and jump into a better way of doing sales.

The first secret of sales is: You aren't succeeding because you're caught in a sales maytag. But the truth can set you free.

SECRET #1

**It's not you that's broken.
It's the system.**

@CheriTree #WhyTheyBuy

CHAPTER 2

THE NEW REALITY: EVERYONE IS IN SALES

"I have always said that everyone is in sales. Maybe you don't hold the title of salesperson, but if the business you are in requires you to deal with people, you, my friend, are in sales."

—Zig Ziglar

Before I delve deeper into telling you how to increase sales, let's first define what "sales" really is. As obvious as the definition may seem, sales encompasses more aspects than most people realize. Sales is *any* interaction where one person makes an offer and convinces another person to accept it. Sure, I could sell you an apple at a farmer's market in a traditionally recognized sales situation, but then it would be your job to sell your child on the idea of eating that apple instead of a cookie.

So long as you are making an offer and the case for acceptance, you are engaging in sales. If you have ever tried to convince someone to see or do things your way, you are a salesperson.

Simply put, sales skills equal influence. Whether you're the traditional salesperson selling a product or service, an employee selling your idea to your peer group, a leader selling your vision to your followers, a corporate executive selling your forecasts to your shareholders, a fundraiser selling your non-profit campaign to your donors, a lover selling your dream vacation to your spouse, a parent selling your child on why he should eat his vegetables, or a Girl Scout selling cookies—the fact of the matter is—you're in sales!

MY EARLY START IN SALES

Ironically, I got my first start in sales when I was nine years old in the Girl Scouts. I was living in the Upper Peninsula of Michigan where my dad was stationed at an Air Force Base. I had to ask my mom to drive me to each potential customer's home because we lived miles away from our neighbors. I loved the thrill of closing the sale and collecting money for those cookies—even though I never got to keep any of the profits. But, at the time, I was just as thrilled about winning the contest for selling the most cookies as I was about making money.

This early success put me on the path to becoming an entrepreneur. My next adventure was having my own lemonade stand—this time I could keep the money I made! I remember spending countless hours parked outside my home in Utah with my twin brothers selling cups of lemonade for ten cents each. My mom made us pay for the products we used to make the lemonade, and after a full day of selling, I only netted about thirty cents, and I had to split that with my brothers. That sucked! At that point, I realized I couldn't keep 100 percent of the revenue since I had to pay for inventory and labor, so I quickly came to the conclusion I needed to find a better way to make money than selling lemonade.

My next opportunity to make money appeared while I was in the seventh grade and living in Hawaii. My first year there, I didn't live on the military base where the kids got picked up for school by the bus. Instead, I either walked to school or got dropped off by my parents. Before I'd get to school, I would pass a candy truck that was parked right off the school property, selling its assortment of candies to kids just like me! I had a sweet tooth and would often buy a few pieces of candy from the truck—Now and Laters, Pixie Stix, Astro Pops, or Jolly Rancher sticks. Our school had a rule that if you were bussed to school, you were not allowed to leave campus, which meant most kids could not buy candy from the truck—and that equaled opportunity for me! My classmates started to offer to buy my private stash of candy off me for a lot more than what I had paid for it. Each day, I'd buy more and more candy from the candy truck and sell it for a premium, making several dollars of profit in a few hours. This was fun!

Then one day, my grandpa came to visit and I shared with him my success story. Since he owned a candy factory, he suggested that instead of buying my candy from the candy truck, I'd be better off buying it directly from the wholesaler! He helped me research where the candy wholesaler was on the island and took me there. It was the most magical day of my life! I walked inside the A.C. Lyau company warehouse and saw rows and rows of candy! Every type of candy I could ever dream of having was stocked in this warehouse—it was like being inside Willy Wonka's factory!

I bought my first few cases of Jolly Rancher sticks and headed to school the next day with my backpack filled with candy instead of books! Each Jolly Rancher stick cost me seven-and-a-half cents and I sold it for twenty-five cents. I started selling them hand over fist and would bring home piles of cash each day from school! Selling candy was more fun than anything I was learning in school, and I was quickly nicknamed the "Candy Girl" on campus. I sold candy for the next few years, until we moved halfway around the world.

As I finished my second year of high school, my dad was relocated to Tunisia, Africa, for a two-year diplomatic assignment to work at the American Embassy. There were no English-speaking schools in Tunisia, so my two twin brothers and I were shipped off to a military boarding school in

London, England. My dad flew there with us and got me all checked into my dorm where I'd be living for the next two years until I graduated. The very first thing I noticed was that there were no vending machines in the dorms. A lightbulb turned on in my head! When I asked the staff members working there whether it would be okay if I sold a few things from my dorm room, they said "Yes"! No one had ever asked to do this before—so I got to be the first!

While all the students were getting settled into their dorm rooms and becoming acclimated to living away from home, I was busy rearranging my furniture so I could turn my room into a mini 7-Eleven convenience store! I went to the military base and stocked up on supplies—chips, soda, snacks, popcorn—all the munchies you'd want if you were trapped in a dorm with no food or drinks available between meals.

For the next two years, I ran the best snack store on campus, pulling in thousands of dollars in revenue, which allowed me to pay for my basketball shoes, several school trips to France and Belgium, and to save money for college.

When I went to college, things got more challenging. There were vending machines everywhere, and I needed to find my next opportunity to make money. I had to pay for my own education, so I got a couple of part-time jobs, working at the campus creamery scooping ice cream for $3.60 per hour and at Little Caesar's Pizza on nights and weekends for $4.25 per hour. Minimum wage sucked, so I started looking for ways to make more money, but the only options were sales jobs. I thought I was pretty good in sales based on my past experiences, so I went for it—and failed miserably!

I tried selling Cutco knives, but I never sold one, except for the starter kit to myself. I still think they're the best knives in the world! Then I tried selling Mary Kay cosmetics, which was another miserable failure, and to make it worse, my friends laughed at me—I was a total tomboy and didn't even wear makeup! I tried selling water filters, but I didn't even have a home to use them in, so I never sold one.

I later got hired to work in a call center on full commission and had to make cold calls to find people who wanted to buy the company's products—I only closed one sale. That job didn't last long.

Back to the drawing board I went! Maybe I wasn't cut out for sales on a professional level after all? How could something I loved so much be so frustrating? There seemed to be an art to the sales process that I didn't grasp, so I decided to focus on my education and prepare myself for a professional career with a salary. The idea of having an executive salary sounded good...at least for a while. But my real passion was to be an entrepreneur, and therefore, I needed to learn how to sell at the professional level.

WHAT DOES SALES MEAN FOR THE MODERN PROFESSIONAL?

Sales is part of everything we do.

One in every nine people works directly in sales.

@U.S. Bureau of Labor Statistics #WhyTheyBuy

This makes sales the largest profession in the U.S.—reason enough for sales to matter to the average businessperson. However, even people in non-sales jobs require sales skills to achieve professional success. A radical shift in the marketplace has put everyone in sales.

That's because, at its core, selling is simply using your power of influence to impact the decisions made by another person. Professional salespeople aren't the only ones who perform behaviors traditionally associated with sales. Anyone can use powerful sales tactics to improve his or her perception, effectiveness at work, and life. Modern professionals need sales skills to make an impact on their world and promote their views.

I may have a background in sales, but some of my most challenging sales have had nothing to do with traditional sales roles; they've been about selling my ideas to other people. When I was first building my company around B.A.N.K., every day felt like a high-stakes sales situation—because it was. I had to get key stakeholders to buy into my vision, or risk seeing my business fall apart—or even worse, fail to launch.

EVERY PERSON IN EVERY CAREER PARTICIPATES IN SALES EVERY DAY

If you think you can find a profession where you can avoid selling, think again. Every day, managers persuade teams on a plan for success, lawyers persuade juries to side with their clients, politicians persuade the electorate to embrace new legislature, and entrepreneurs persuade the world on their next big ideas. Even in jobs far from sales, persuasion is a daily fact of life. Teachers must convince students to listen and learn. Doctors must convince patients to take care of their health. Even parents must convince kids to wash their faces and brush their teeth.

In fact, a study by Dan Pink, author of *To Sell Is Human*, shows people in non-sales professions spend 40 percent of their time at work persuading others. Reflect back on your last few interactions at work. There's a good chance that at least one required you to persuade a coworker or supervisor about something. You use sales to make your point—or fail at sales, leading to your opinion being shot down.

We are continuously putting forth ideas that we need others to agree with and act upon. Whether you are mediating a conflict between coworkers, recruiting a colleague to pursue your course of action, asking your boss for a raise, or simply advocating for what you know is true, you are constantly attempting to influence others.

WE ALL NEED SALES

For many professionals, especially those who are not dedicated salespeople, the idea of being in sales can feel unsettling. For them, the idea of "selling" the people in their lives on the ideas and strategies important to them can feel deceptive or unsavory. I hope, however, that since you're reading this book, you already know better. The days of the "used car salesman" tactics are long gone. Salesmanship doesn't have a negative connotation.

According to the old stereotype, salespeople are manipulative, insincere, and focused solely on closing a sale. Not only is this stereotyped antiquated; frankly, it's wrong. With the sheer amount of easily accessible information over the Internet and a hyper-competitive market, influence gained based on "tricks" would never be very effective or long-lasting. Remember, people hate to be sold—but they love to buy!

In today's economy, it's more important than ever before that salespeople are honest, transparent, and provide discernible value to their clients. As author and top sales consultant Bob Burg says,

"All things being equal, people will do business with and refer business to those people they know, like, and trust."

– Bob Burg #WhyTheyBuy

Influence and trust go hand-in-hand. You can't have one without the other. Sales success depends not on tricking anyone, but rather gaining influence with them by knowing how to communicate your message effectively. By maintaining your integrity, you can dramatically expand your influence and success.

There really is no debate. Whether you're an entrepreneur, an employee, a business owner, a corporate executive, a pharmaceutical sales rep, a network marketer, a consultant, a spouse, a parent, or even a Girl Scout, you are in sales! The question is simply whether you are good at it or not.

It's time to ask yourself, "Am I skilled at influencing others?" Now that you realize your ability to influence others determines your level of professional success and impacts the quality of your life, you also should realize that selling effectively isn't just something that can give your life a small boost; it can change your life dramatically for the better. The second secret of sales is that we are all in sales. Thus, it's imperative in business that you must do well in sales if you want to survive and thrive. It's time to embrace it and master it—if you want to be in it to win it!

SECRET #2

We are all in sales!

@CheriTree #WhyTheyBuy

CHAPTER 3

SALES IS NOT A NUMBERS GAME

"All business is a people business."

– Brian Tracy

You've likely heard countless times that "Sales is a numbers game," just like you've heard "In order to get more yeses, you've got to get more nos." This advice is repeated so often that it seems almost sacrilegious to question it. But what if these statements are just myths? What if it's this exact advice that holds so many salespeople back and costs companies millions of dollars in lost market share and revenue?

If you are a business owner or salesperson who still believes that sales is a numbers game, then you are selling yourself short. While you might get sales if you present to enough people, you can't win them all. Closing each individual sale isn't viable with the typical sales approach. When you say, "Sales is a numbers game," you are essentially saying that you lack the skills and training to control the outcome of each sales situation.

THE "SALES IS A NUMBERS GAME" MYTH

Thankfully, the logic of "getting more yeses" is flawed. The fact is, in order to get more yeses, you just need to get more yeses, not more nos. This is just common sense! It's the number of your successes that matters, not the number of your failures.

The "numbers game" myth is used by those who trust in luck and chance to close sales; this method is like throwing spaghetti noodles against the wall and hoping some of them stick, or betting your chips at the craps table. It decreases your chance of success and makes sales harder than necessary because it requires you to waste all your energy getting nos. Essentially, you spin your wheels getting hundreds or even thousands of nos, making you too tired to keep searching for the yeses.

Selling according to the numbers game myth is like trying to win a skeet-shooting competition by simply shooting a bunch of bullets into the sky and hoping for the best. Sure, you may hit some clay pigeons, but you're going to waste a bunch of time, resources, and energy in the process. It's better to target each effort toward a single clay pigeon with careful aim and specialized strategy. You've got to pick your target and your moment carefully and modify your strategy accordingly. You may still not hit every target, but you'll at least have a better chance at success every time you shoot.

Sales is the same. If you're just selling to everyone you meet with no consideration for who your prospects are, what their needs are, or why they buy, you aren't setting yourself up to win. You'll probably still make some sales (and maybe even a lot of sales if you're willing to burn the candle at both ends and wear yourself out chasing the maximum number of prospects possible), but you'll waste a lot of time, resources, and energy in the process. A strategic approach and understanding of why they buy lets you close more sales faster without wearing you out expending fruitless sales effort.

CHANGING THE OUTDATED "DIALING FOR DOLLARS" NUMBERS-BASED SALES GAME

If you've been in sales long enough, you're surely familiar with cold calling, or "dialing for dollars" as my bosses liked to call it. The concept is simple. You reach out to 100 unqualified prospects at random, give them your standard sales presentation as fast as possible, and hope to get at least one or two of them to the next step in the sales process. I remember several times opening a phone book and calling random people just to hit my numbers. What a nightmare!

Cold calling is ineffective and, for most salespeople, excruciating. Neither the salesperson nor the prospect comes away with a good feeling about most calls. Most of the time people would hang up on me, or even worse—yell at me and tell me never to call them again. Ugh!

Then, since you didn't get nearly enough people to the next step, you've got to do the whole thing all over again. And then again. Repeat, repeat, repeat until rich—or so they'd say.

It's no surprise that the churn rate for the average sales team is about 25 percent per year, with dropout rates as high as 50 and even 60 percent considered normal in sales. The average salesperson only lasts about two years before leaving the field entirely. After all, how long can someone keep hearing "No" without giving up?

In network marketing, the numbers are even worse! The average sales rep typically quits within the first ninety days, creating an enormous turnover in the organization and untold frustration that ripples throughout the entire industry. What a shame. I applaud those who have the courage to build a home-based business—they deserve to win too.

Sales as a numbers game requires a "survival of the fittest" attitude. Only those willing to face a large amount of demoralizing failure and ruthless rejection every day can possibly stay in the game. Only the strongest stick it out, and only a few really thrive.

After a few short years in corporate America, I read *Rich Dad Poor Dad* and was ready to give the sales world another shot. I chose to become a financial advisor and needed to build my own book of business. Here is where I learned a lot more about the numbers game.

I was almost a casualty of this method myself. I hated dialing for dollars—mostly because it didn't actually get me many dollars! Then I decided to modify my approach a bit. Every person on our team was supposed to get ten prospects a day. ("Ten a day keeps the bill collector away!" they'd say). Since I wasn't doing as well as I needed to on the phone, I resolved to talk to as many people as I could in person. I used to go out to malls, restaurants near big workplaces, and other public places to talk to prospects.

My strategy each day was simple. I would start out with ten pennies in my left pocket. Each time I got a new prospect, I would move a penny to my right pocket. I couldn't go home until I had transferred all ten pennies.

Sounds easy, right? Unfortunately, I still didn't have much success. Although the in-person approach made the whole experience a little better (no one hung up on me!), I was still striking out most of the time. The idea that sales was a numbers game was haunting me. I had moments where I sat in my car bawling my eyes out because of the fear and frustration of cold prospecting.

I remember sitting in the mall one day while working up the courage to talk to a prospect—a RadioShack manager. Knowing I had to go in there with an agenda made me feel a pit in my stomach. I wasn't going into the store to buy something or even to make friends; I was going in there to give my standard presentation and hopefully make some money off of him. It wasn't a nice feeling.

That was the day I decided to make a change. I wanted to reverse-engineer the sales process and find a better way to sell, which meant that I needed to understand *why they buy*. I wanted to be able to keep my integrity and make the sales process better for both of us. I wanted to get out of the numbers game and find a way to close more sales without cutthroat and ineffective tactics. I knew that the numbers game simply didn't work...but what would?

IF SALES ISN'T A NUMBERS GAME, WHAT KIND OF GAME IS IT?

Once I dedicated myself to updating the way I sold, I knew I had to play a new game. But which one? If sales is not a numbers game, what kind of game is it? Here's a clue....

Brian Tracy, best-selling author and business coach, says,

> **"All business is a people business."**
>
> **– Brian Tracy #WhyTheyBuy**

Richard Branson, billionaire entrepreneur, says, "When it comes to business, it's all about people, people, people."

We've talked about this concept already; it's the basis of the first two secrets. The source of influence and the essence of making sales lies not in numbers but in people. We have to understand people in order to understand how to get the "Yes." It's not about repeating the same presentation over and over as many times as possible in order to make the numbers tip in your favor thanks to sheer volume. It's about customizing your approach to each person and responding to your prospect's unique needs to make the sale, based on the science of *why they buy*.

HOW SMART SALESPEOPLE LIKE YOU CAN WIN THE SALES GAME

Too many salespeople think that if they cast a wide enough net, they're bound to catch someone. While you may close a few sales that way, such a needle-in-a-haystack approach is still just a bad approach.

People want to do business with someone who has their best interests in mind, not someone who is just playing the numbers game. When you instead play the people game and understand *why they buy*, you make it clear to people that you care about their needs by giving them an offer that suits their unique business challenges and current situation. With the numbers game, you carefully have to count every single meeting, conversation, sales presentation, and interaction with others, hoping to hit your goals and build up the sales numbers you want. With this new approach, the only numbers you ever have to worry about are the large numbers in your bank account!

The goal should be to strengthen your people skills so your success rate increases, not to increase your overall volume in the vain hope that some people will say yes. When you focus on selling using your new B.A.N.K. skills with your prospects, you will begin to see great numbers every time—and that's money you can take to the bank.

Are you ready to let go of the numbers game myth? I promise you'll get better results than any other traditional sales training will provide you. The truth is, the more I studied traditional sales training, the more I got ordinary results. When I shifted my focus to studying more about people, I got extraordinary results. This secret was a game-changer for me! If you want to succeed in sales, you've got to shift your focus, too. Sales is all about people, not numbers.

SECRET #3

Sales is not a numbers game; it's a people game!

@CheriTree #WhyTheyBuy

CHAPTER 4

IS SELLING AN ART OR A SCIENCE?

> **"Art is a lie that makes us realize truth."**
>
> **– Pablo Picasso**

The first secret revealed that it's not you, it's the system that is broken. Our second secret established that we are all in sales all the time, and our third secret revealed that sales is not a numbers game—which makes our next secret about sales even more important. If we are all participating in sales all the time and it's not a numbers game—what is it and how do we master it?

I pursued a career in sales as a financial advisor because I loved the topic of money and thought the sales would come easily to me. I was wrong! Selling people on the idea of letting me invest their money was a lot harder than I thought! I knew I had to be excellent at sales if I wanted to build a successful career, and the experts surely had the answers.

I spent thousands of dollars and countless hours on sales coaching and training. In many ways, this training helped me a lot, but there was a phrase that sales experts stated regularly that frustrated me every time: "Selling is an art you need to master." What did they mean by art? I felt so annoyed every time I heard someone say that. If selling is some complicated mixture of artistic skill and innate ability, how could everyone possibly master it? After all, I was not an artist! Not that many can say that they are.

IS SELLING AN ART?

Is selling really an art? Many experts seem to think so. In reality, few sales coaches spend much time thinking about the answer at all. Selling has to be an art, right? It's obviously not a pure science, like physics or chemistry. So why think about it at all?

Unlike my trainers, however, I couldn't stop thinking about it. Science has come a long way in the past fifty, ten, or even five years. Now we can accurately forecast thousands of things we never even dreamt we could use science to predict. Today, all sorts of disciplines from linguistics to human behavior can be analyzed using the scientific method.

Maybe selling isn't an art after all—and if selling is a science, accurately answering this question becomes vital for our sales success.

There's a problem with the assumption that selling is an art. Whether selling is ultimately an art or a science isn't just a theoretical musing. The reality of selling—and your understanding of this reality—has a measurable impact on how successfully you actually sell.

THE PROBLEM WITH "SELLING IS AN ART"

If selling really is an art, not a science, then selling can't be done well by everyone.

@CheriTree #WhyTheyBuy

After all, anyone can follow science-based instructions to get a proven result, but the odds of being a master in the field of art are much smaller, which explains why there are so many "starving artists."

Think about the difference. I can study painting for thirty years and never be as amazing as Michelangelo unless I have that special something that makes me that kind of artist. I may enjoy exercising my creativity on occasion, but master painter I am not. It doesn't matter how hard I work, I'm simply not going to paint the Sistine Chapel.

I can, however, learn a scientific formula and use it successfully with enough practice. I'm not going to lie; science was not my favorite subject as a student. It could be boring at times, and I wasn't always the best at using complex formulas to get results to abstract chemistry problems that I felt would have no impact on my life. But I always appreciated that with the right formula, anyone can get the same results using science.

In chemistry, if you put the right ingredients together in the right proportions and in the right order, you get the results you want every single time. I did enjoy making potions in class and always held my breath every time I'd mix different things together—hoping nothing would explode! The fact that I had an exact recipe made it much easier to duplicate my teacher's results. Ultimately, I didn't need to be a rocket scientist to do my homework, so I realized anyone could master it. I can be a successful chemist with enough study and practice, and so can you.

Therefore, determining whether selling is an art or a science would allow me to predict how successful I could be at it. If selling were an art, I might never become a top salesperson. If selling were a science, however, I just had to learn the right formula and get good at using it. There would be a right approach that could get me better results every time. (And believe me, I was much more motivated to use the science of sales to increase my income than I was ever motivated to master chemistry—although I do know the periodic symbol for gold!)

Since we are all in sales, selling as an art is a challenge. Some people are simply destined to be good at sales and to succeed, while the rest of us probably never will. Studies show that the best salesperson outsells the average salesperson 57:1. If selling is an art, those top performers were simply the Michelangelos and Picassos of the sales world, born to succeed.

Since I hadn't managed to reach my goal of a six (and then seven!) figure income in my first five years as a financial advisor, I was worried that if selling is an art, I would never be on top. I wasn't a master in training; I was just someone who could do a "good enough" job. If selling is a science, on the other hand, those top performers simply know the right strategy for selling more—and I could learn it!

IF SELLING IS REALLY INFLUENCE, IS INFLUENCE AN ART OR A SCIENCE?

Clearly, the answer to this question is much more important than those trainers realized. We need to determine whether selling is an art or a science to figure out how best to master sales. So how do we figure out which label is correct? We have to get to the core of the issue.

Remember, sales is about influence. If sales equals influence, the question we really have to answer becomes, "Is influence an art or a science?" Luckily, it's an easy question to answer.

If you look up "the science of influence" online, you'll likely find tens of thousands of blogs, articles, books, and websites. Psychologists and behavioral economists have investigated this subject thoroughly, and today, you can easily find many of the factors scientists have proven affect your influence and powers of persuasion.

CHANGING THE WAY WE LOOK AT INFLUENCE

It wasn't always so easy, though. For thousands of years, influence was considered an art. Some people were simply better at influencing others, and no one really questioned why. It was generally assumed that money and social position were the only factors that could reliably affect influence. Other factors were simply an art with which the lucky were gifted.

Around the turn of the twentieth century, this all changed. Psychologists decided it was time for a thorough investigation of the factors involved in creating influence—systematically, methodically, and scientifically. These studies revealed plenty of proven ways to increase a person's influence. In fact, these studies were getting such impressive results and attracting so much attention that the science of influence became its own discipline—social psychology.

Social psychology is generally defined as the study of how people influence each other—which makes it a very powerful topic to study to improve sales success. It has revealed verbal and nonverbal cues that may improve any message's appeal. It has helped people communicate better. It even has distilled influence into several simple formulas that anyone can use successfully.

Of all the areas of psychology, influence has been one of the most thoroughly researched and demystified. Social psychologists have even paired with other types of psychologists, such as personality theorists, to get a deeper understanding of the ways our personality traits impact our influence. Moreover, they've paired with other scientific disciplines, such as behavioral economics and linguistics, to get the broadest understanding of influence possible.

Anyone can replicate the scientific principles of influence to get better results. No matter how poorly you naturally influence others, you can now leverage science to enhance your influence in any situation using simple, proven, and replicable strategies.

@CheriTree #WhyTheyBuy

WHY YOU SHOULD CARE ABOUT THE SCIENCE OF SALES

Clearly, there is a science behind influencing others. If influence is a science, so is sales. This discovery changed my outlook on sales dramatically. After all, science can be mastered by nearly *anyone*. I always believed I could reach the top of the sales game, and now I knew where to find the tools to get me there, thanks to the science of sales.

When I discovered the secret that sales is a science, I realized I could be one of those top performers. I could make millions, achieve real wealth, live the lifestyle I always wanted, and find security for myself and my family. I just had to learn the science.

Unfortunately, the science of sales was elusive. All the experts I had been counting on for answers kept insisting that selling was an art. I had to go looking for the science myself, struggling every step of the way. Sure, I eventually figured out the science of selling by looking at the science of influence and using my own experiments (experiments that ultimately allowed me to develop B.A.N.K.), but it wasn't easy. The old myth of the art of sales held me back every time because I didn't know how to master it—and the type of art I created in the sales world usually looked like refrigerator art from your five-year-old!

To use the chicken-and-the-egg scenario of which comes first, selling is first a science, and then it can be considered an art. Too many sales coaches and trainers overlook this key fact. It's a terrible missed opportunity. If more people taught the science of selling rather than assumptions based on their own "art," fewer people would be forced to struggle against the sales maytag we too often find ourselves caught inside, drowning in failure and rejection.

USING THE SCIENCE OF SALES TO MAKE FINE ART

The fourth secret to sales shouldn't really be considered a secret at all. In fact, it's so widely available that everyone should know it: selling is a science. That doesn't mean that a master salesperson can't turn his own sales presentations into works of art we can all admire. It means that you can actually learn how to paint like Picasso—even if you're simply painting by numbers.

It's said that a really good salesperson can make a sale without a prospect even feeling like they've been sold. From far away, sales looks like art. What the untrained eye can't see is the careful strategy behind every step of the sale. It's like looking at a paint-by-number portrait. The painter was given a simple step-by-step formula for each color choice and brushstroke. The end result may be breathtaking, but scientific method guided every action that propelled the painter to the end result. We look at the finished painting and think the painter had some mystical artistic skills, but he just followed a formula. Anyone could do the same and get the same results—all you have to do is paint by numbers.

Selling is exactly the same. To the untrained eye, the best salespeople look like master artists, but they just know what strategies work. They have somehow figured out the science behind massive sales success—often from years of trial and error—which makes top producers hard to duplicate. The good news is that this book will reveal the science you need to become a top producer or duplicate your top producers, and achieve record sales! You can use science to create what looks like art—and in sales that means game-changing results.

You don't have to be a charismatic, natural salesperson from day one to achieve massive success—and even if you are, you can increase your sales dramatically with the application of the right science. All you need is a scientific understanding of *why they buy* to ensure your success.

SECRET #4

Selling is only an art if you know the science!

@CheriTree #WhyTheyBuy

**"Success is a science;
if you have the conditions,
you get the result."**

— Oscar Wilde

SECTION 2: THE SCIENCE

In Section 1, we unlocked four very important secrets to increasing your sales that can position you on the right path for significant growth. The fact that the system is broken and we're all in sales—the first two secrets—makes the other two even more important. After all, sales now is the primary task of every entrepreneur—and person, including you.

But perhaps more importantly, our four secrets show you how to succeed in sales without getting stuck in the sales maytag despite the system being rigged against you. It's important to remember that sales is not a numbers game; it's a *people* game. You need to understand people if you truly want to understand sales—and in order to understand people—you need to understand science.

So where should you start looking for the most relevant scientific truths? That's where the fourth secret comes in: selling is a science, and as such, there is a proven, right way to go about increasing your sales. You don't have to be a certain kind of person to succeed in sales, either. With the right tools, anyone can master the sales process—including you!

Of course, the science of sales won't do you much good unless you understand what that science says. Over the years, scientists, business analysts, and behavioral economists have conducted thousands of research studies investigating what makes a salesperson successful and what factors predict a better close rate. It would be impossible for any single salesperson to learn, much less apply, all the lessons these studies have revealed.

Nothing reveals more core truths about communication better than linguistics, and nothing explains human behavior better than psychology. That's why we focus our discoveries on revelations in personality science in these disciplines. In this section, I'm going to show you the science that tells us how to create influence during the sales process and how to communicate more effectively. I'll teach you how to convert psychology to buyology, and how personality science influences buying decisions. Most importantly, I'll show you how to use that science to close more sales faster—based on proven science that reveals *why they buy*.

CHAPTER 5

PERSONALITY SCIENCE

"It is more important to know what sort of person has a disease than to know what sort of disease a person has."

— Hippocrates

Once I realized that sales was a science, I started studying all the factors involved in influence. I was quickly overwhelmed. There is almost too much information in the field to digest!

Luckily, I knew sales is ultimately a people game, which allowed me to hone in on the factors of influence in psychology (the area of science that reveals the most useful secrets about the way people think). My fascination with studying more about people led me to personality theory. Personality theory and personality science explore the ways people are different (and the same) according to innate characteristics.

I'm going to take you on a short journey back in time so that you can understand the origin of personality theory and the development of the science over the past couple of thousand years. This will help you understand the evolution of personality science and also why it is applicable to sales in this day and age.

PERSONALITY SCIENCE AND SALES

There are a number of frameworks in personality science that can predict certain behaviors, preferences, and abilities based on some sort of personality type categorization. Some, for example, explore a person's sociability. Others focus on task orientation or neuroticism. Essentially, personality science looks to explain why we do things based on our various personality traits.

After studying existing science-based personality typing systems in depth, I created B.A.N.K. rooted in the principles of personality science. Rather than predicting stress behaviors or sociability or anything else explained by personality types, B.A.N.K. predicts buying behavior, finally answering *why they buy.*

In sales, the Holy Grail would be an ability to predict why someone buys, so personality science is the perfect place to start if you want to succeed in sales.

@CheriTree #WhyTheyBuy

Of course, personality science is nothing new. It dates back thousands of years to Hippocrates, the Greek physician who is also known as the "father of modern medicine." While B.A.N.K. codes may be revolutionary, the personality science it is based on was proven long ago, and it would be impossible to understand the B.A.N.K. methodology's significance without a basic understanding of this science. Before we explain the B.A.N.K. system, let's time travel back twenty-four hundred years so you can understand a little more about the origins and history of personality types.

THE FOUR TEMPERAMENTS

Around 400 B.C., the Greek physician Hippocrates developed the idea of the four temperaments. His idea was simple: four fundamental personality types exist, and each type needs to be medically treated differently. Under the framework of the four temperaments developed by Hippocrates (and fleshed out by later students like Galen), each person was either:

1. sanguine: characterized as optimistic and social
2. choleric: characterized as short-tempered or irritable
3. melancholic: characterized as analytical and quiet
4. phlegmatic: characterized as relaxed and peaceful
5. some mixture of the four

Hippocrates emphasized that we each have the characteristics of all four types to some degree.

As Hippocrates understood it, the balance of the four humors—the bodily fluids blood (red), urine (yellow), black bile (or blue), and phlegm (green)—caused people to have different primary personality traits (the colors associated with the bodily fluids show the origins of colors associated with personality typing). To treat illness or minimize unpleasant personality traits, Hippocrates suggested restoring balance between the humors by removing the offending ones. Of course, medicine has come a long way since then. It's generally accepted that the humors of the body and our personalities don't really have anything to do with treating disease—and you can't get rid of someone's irritating qualities by bleeding them. Still, the four temperaments remain relevant in personality science.

The proto-psychological theory of the four temperaments forms the basis of many personality typing systems today. Most personality psychologists recognize the traits of each temperament to be the most important characteristics in predicting behavior (although the names and explanations vary). In fact, these four basic personality types often correspond directly with the most popular personality types talked about in today's business world.

THE EVOLUTION OF PERSONALITY SCIENCE

So, how did the popular personality types today develop out of the four temperaments? It took a long time to get to where we are now. For centuries, no one really questioned the four temperaments. However, major physicians, philosophers, and psychologists from Avicenna and Nicholas Culpeper to Immanuel Kant, Rudolf Steiner, and Erich Fromm contributed to our understanding of the four temperaments, giving them more depth and practical application.

Eventually, in the twentieth century, Hans Eysenck did the first major factor-analysis study on differences in personality traits, specifically measuring neuroticism and extraversion. His results validated personality science for the first time using modern scientific methods—and the types that consistently emerged corresponded directly with the personality types suggested by Hippocrates long ago.

After Eysenck's success, more personality scientists started to research other dimensions of behavior that could be explained by building upon these categories. Temperaments and factors that correlated with the types they had come to represent were mapped against specific behaviors and roles to predict more facets of people's lives. Essentially, universal traits originally ascribed to the four temperaments were recategorized into better-defined and more efficient personality typing systems, such as the Keirsey Temperament Sorter.

Eventually, measuring the personality traits associated with the temperaments themselves was rejected in favor of measuring other personality traits like the Big Five or Jung's Four Functions. Personality tests and assessments like DiSC, the Myers Briggs Type Indicator (MBTI), and the Sixteen Personality Factor Assessment (16PF) were developed to measure such traits. The temperaments stopped being considered the only way of typing people, but remain an important analogy due to their accurate use in predicting human behavior.

PERSONALITY TESTS AND ASSESSMENTS

Fast forward to today, and hundreds of different personality type tests and assessments have been developed to predict and describe our behavior. Popular assessments include the MBTI, DiSC, Color Codes, Management Drives, Enneagrams, 16PF, StrengthsFinder, Insights, Birkman Method, Kolbe Index, and many, many others. The list could go on for pages.

When you look up personality tests, you can find one based around pretty much any theme you can imagine, and each claims to reveal endless types of personality insights. I've come across personality categories from these assessments based on animals, sea creatures, astrology signs, jewels, Chinese elements, colors, and even types of love. You name it—I've seen it! While some of these are more scientific and useful than others, there are limitless options when it comes to personality assessments today.

Millions of people have taken some form of questionnaire or other standardized test to reveal aspects of their characters or psychological makeups and learn more about themselves. People enjoy the insights they discover by looking deeper into their innate personalities.

In fact, you probably are familiar with at least a few personality assessments yourself. You may have even taken one or two. Even if you've never been particularly interested in learning more about yourself, you've probably heard about them in an educational or professional setting. Eighty percent of Fortune 500 companies use some personality assessment for training, hiring, or team development purposes—and according to Deloitte, the majority of companies specifically use personality tests to assess the likelihood of prospective candidates' future success. If you've ever applied for a job in the corporate world or worked for a major company, you've likely heard personality types discussed.

MY OWN JOURNEY TO UNDERSTANDING PERSONALITY SCIENCE

When I was starting out as a financial advisor, I was determined to succeed, despite a lack of experience or expertise in the field. I knew success would require lots of training, which is why I started attending extra company trainings nearly every week. Most of these trainings had to do directly with financial services and the products we were selling, but one week, a few months into starting my business, the focus was a little different.

An expert had been brought in to teach us about personality types and how we could leverage our own personality type to improve our sales. I was fascinated. I had previously taken a few personality assessments and loved learning about myself, but I had never considered using personality science to improve my sales. The idea was pretty exciting. I could learn all about my favorite topic—me!—and improve my career as a financial advisor. Cool!

That day, I listened in rapt attention to the speaker, and after I left, I dedicated myself to learning as much as I could about every personality typing system out there. I was sure that if I learned enough about communicating better with people, I could improve my sales. After all, this was my first year in the business, and I wasn't doing so well.

THE PROBLEM WITH USING PERSONALITY SCIENCE SUCCESSFULLY IN SALES

Admittedly, when I took my first few assessments, I was fascinated about what I learned about myself. I read pages and pages of all kinds of insights these assessments provided to me, and it was very cool. However, my fascination quickly turned into frustration when I realized that not one of these assessments ever made me more money! Not one of them ever helped me close more sales. Not one of them ever helped me get a yes instead of a no. Never once did they teach me *why they buy*!

I grew more and more irritated and increasingly frustrated. As years passed, I improved my sales incrementally, but I was never able to get the big results I thought personality science promised. After five years in the business, I was tens of thousands of dollars in credit card debt trying to learn how to be successful in sales, while still making only about $72,000 a year. I felt like I was living the definition of insanity, trying to figure out how to significantly improve my sales to no avail.

What was the point of all these assessments if they couldn't solve my challenges, close my sales, and pay my bills? Something seemed to be missing. Then one day I thought,

If it's been proven for centuries that people are different, could that mean they buy differently?

@CheriTree #WhyTheyBuy

The lightbulb turned on, and I realized I had just discovered the missing link.

CHAPTER 6

THE MISSING LINK

"The very essence of instinct is that it's followed independently of reason."

– Charles Darwin

When it came to sales and personality science, I felt there had to be a missing link. Something was just out of reach that would allow me finally to connect all the dots and leverage what I had learned.

In biology, *missing link* is a casual term for any transitional fossil or species that helps scientists understand the connection between two better-known species. An example would be the chimpanzee. It's the closest living mammal with a common ancestor to humans. Studying chimpanzees has helped scientists better understand human evolution because the commonalities and differences between humans and chimpanzees provide answers to key questions about our origins, linking ideas and insights.

In other words, the missing link is a key missing piece of the puzzle that can solve a lot of unanswered questions. To connect everything I had learned through personality science with practical applications in the sales process, I needed to find a new kind of missing link—one that would provide salespeople answers in *buyology*, the science of buying behavior.

WHAT WAS MISSING IN PERSONALITY SCIENCE AND BUYOLOGY

After all, what I really cared about in learning personality science was how it influenced buying behavior. I didn't care so much about the psychology, like whether my prospects were introverts or extroverts. I just cared about how they made their buying decisions, what specifically triggered the yes or the no response, and ultimately, *why they buy.* It's not like my personality type has ever come up directly during a sales call. I mean, really...what customer cares what my personality type is in the sales process? I've never gone on a sales call where my customer said, "Cheri, before you give us your presentation, I'd just like to know your personality type."

Has that ever happened to you? The answer is most likely "No." I had always assumed that knowing my own personality type would help me give a more effective sales presentation…but then it occurred to me—maybe I should know my customer's personality type instead!

What if I could know all the revealing insights available through personality science about my customer, and not just myself? Then I could customize my presentation according to his or her personality type, not mine. After all, the customer ultimately makes the buying decision, not me. It was an important Aha! moment. If people are different, shouldn't they *buy* differently? And if so, how could I sell to each personality type more effectively?

I needed something brand new. Something outside the box. So I set out to develop a personality typing system that would provide the missing link and essentially convert psychology into buyology.

@CheriTree #WhyTheyBuy

Suddenly, my passion for personality science was renewed. I began looking for a personality typing system that could teach me how to identify my customer's type and how to sell to each type differently. I searched high and low, but none of the personality programs I could find taught how to crack the personality codes of my prospects, nor how to alter the way I sell to them. It seemed like they were all variations of the same tired idea: understanding yourself better.

DEVELOPING B.A.N.K.

I went through many proven and science-based personality typing assessments and programs and started pulling the values, preferences, behaviors, and customs of each type that might have anything to do with the way that type of individual would buy. I wrote them on hundreds of index cards and then sorted the cards into piles of similar characteristics to see whether I could find a pattern based on buying behavior.

Some of the existing personality profiling systems had contradictions, which required me to scramble everything I had learned into a different order. I noticed that most assessments were based in psychology and forced people into a polarity matrix, which showed that if you were high in X, then you must be low in Y. For example, a person could be either an introvert or an extrovert, but her buying behavior was the same. Or two people might have a very driven type of personality, but their buying behaviors were very different.

After I reviewed all the similarities and contradictions, I started creating my own "buying personality" profiles based on which characteristics seemed most commonly to go together. Since there were too many contradictions using a psychological profile, I needed to use a different baseline as the foundation. I based my system in values, with a hypothesis that people make buying decisions from a core set of values, connected back to personality science.

That's when I started testing. I would ask my clients to choose which of my profiles best described them. I told them that this process would allow me to serve them better and save us both some time. My clients loved the experience and thought it was a fun icebreaker. Once they chose their profile sequence (what later became known as their B.A.N.K. code), I attempted to approach the sales call in a way that best served their associated values.

At first, it didn't always go so well. Some of the profiles were wrong, as were some sales behaviors I tried to use with each type. I had to stumble and fumble my way through it, but I didn't give up. I learned from my mistakes and always asked clients what turned them off or where I had lost the sale. Most of them were happy to give their honest feedback, which I used to modify and adjust the buying personality profiles. With a lot of trial and error (and many lost sales along the way), I developed what would become the B.A.N.K. system.

UNCOVERING THE TRUE MISSING LINK IN BUYOLOGY

My experiment worked! The first year I used B.A.N.K., my income shot up by 695 percent to over a half-million dollars, and within three years, I was earning more than one million dollars a year. I had found the missing link by reverse-engineering personality science to work in sales, and I discovered that at the core of B.A.N.K. was the secret to *why they buy.*

I began to use my own system religiously! I made sure I repeated the process of asking my clients to crack their personality codes, and I began documenting everything I could. I created profile sheets for every client with his or her B.A.N.K. code. I wrote the person's B.A.N.K. code on his or her business card, in my phone, in my CRM, etc. and I began to alter the way I communicated with that person via email, phone calls, meetings, and sales presentations. The B.A.N.K. system was revealing everything I ever wanted to know about *why they buy*, and the yes momentum I got skyrocketed my sales!

For several years, I used the system mostly by myself. I didn't build it originally to teach to anyone else. I built it to help save myself from starving to death as an entrepreneur! But things changed fairly quickly in my third year using the system. I was making a lot of money, winning awards, living a pretty amazing lifestyle, and starting to train a few leaders on duplicating my success. It was working! Some of the people I trained started making hundreds of thousands of dollars annually in their businesses, whereas before, they'd never even earned six figures in a year. Not only did my system work for me, but it was now becoming more and more obvious that it was actually working for others too. This got people excited!

Suddenly, everyone wanted to duplicate my success. I formalized the B.A.N.K. system and started using it in every sales call and interaction I had with clients. After several years, I went on to streamline and systematize B.A.N.K. so I could successfully transfer this key knowledge to anyone who wanted to learn it. I made it duplicable so others would be able to increase their sales and income. I made it more scalable so I could teach it to anyone, anywhere in the world, regardless of their occupation, market, or experience.

More than a decade later, I was honored to work with researchers at top universities in California to validate B.A.N.K. scientifically. A Ph.D. candidate from UC Berkeley partnered with a top professor from San Francisco State University to conduct a series of four studies to test the validity of the B.A.N.K. methodology.

After months of studies, trials, and testing, Dr. Ryan T. Howell, a leading expert in the field of buying behavior and the head researcher on these studies, published the results, proving that

"The B.A.N.K. code assessment is a quick, reliable, and valid measure of personalities that predicts buying behavior and increases your probability of closing the sale."

– Dr. Ryan T. Howell #WhyTheyBuy

He also deemed B.A.N.K. original, meaning it was not a copy of the countless personality-based programs already available in the marketplace.

I didn't set out to add yet another personality test to the field. I just wanted to fill an important gap in the science of selling. What I discovered, however, was far greater than "more of the same." B.A.N.K. was a breakthrough, the true missing link I had been looking for.

If you want to read the white paper on B.A.N.K. published by Dr. Ryan T. Howell, Professor at San Francisco State University, you can download an executive summary or the entire white paper at bankcode.com.

CHAPTER 7

CRACKING THE PERSONALITY CODE

"Poor is the pupil who does not surpass his master."

– Leonardo da Vinci

As I travel around the world and meet a lot of great people, I get asked the same question constantly, "How is B.A.N.K. different from the personality tests I've already taken?"

My answer is simple.

B.A.N.K. is exactly the same—only completely different!

@CheriTree #WhyTheyBuy

While most other personality type assessments are based in psychology, B.A.N.K. is based in buyology—the science of buying behavior.

At the end of the day, that's all that interested me. I didn't care whether my clients were introverts or extroverts, analytical or emotional, or anything else measured by typical personality assessments. What I cared about was cracking the code of *why they buy*.

I was starting to link all the puzzle pieces together, and essentially what I realized is that my B.A.N.K. system would teach me how to *crack the personality code of my customer so that I could take it to the bank!*

Crack the personality code and take it to the bank!

@CheriTree #WhyTheyBuy

THE ANALOGY OF THE CRYPTEX

I'm a huge movie buff! We loved watching movies in my family when I was a kid, and we even had contests to see whether we could identify movies from certain quotes.

When I watched *The Da Vinci Code* movie, something clicked! The entire movie was about "cracking the code" on a device known as a *cryptex*.

The word *cryptex* was coined by Dan Brown in his 2003 novel *The Da Vinci Code*. In the book, the word "cryptex" referred to a portable vault used to hide secret messages. The term combines the words "cryptology" and "codex." *Cryptology* is the study of codes that protect secret information, and a *codex* is an ancient manuscript.

The cryptex featured in the novel is described as a stone cylinder with rotating discs; the discs are inscribed with the letters of the alphabet. The cryptex works much like a combination bicycle lock. Essentially, you twist the discs to spell out the password; when you select the correct password, the lock pops open, allowing you to get inside the inner compartment where the scroll is hidden.

There's a catch, though. The device is booby-trapped. Think of it like a ticking time bomb. The cryptex has an added security feature. The secret information is written on a scroll of thin papyrus wrapped around a vial of vinegar. Papyrus dissolves in vinegar. If you try to force the cryptex open without entering the right password, the fragile glass vial breaks, dissolving the papyrus scroll, and the secret message disappears, never to be read.

In *The Da Vinci Code* storyline, the secret to the Holy Grail was written on the papyrus scroll. Unwilling to risk erasing such valuable information forever, the characters had to get the passcode right. Cracking the code was essential to unlocking the greatest secret in history—just as cracking the personality code is essential to unlocking the greatest success for salespeople in history!

CRACKING THE CODE

Why is *The Da Vinci Code* analogy of the cryptex so important to you? Because it is symbolic of what actually is happening in the sales process with every one of your customers.

Imagine that every one of your prospects, clients, or leads has an invisible cryptex tucked away in his pocket or her purse. Now imagine that what is locked inside this device is a tiny little rolled-up piece of paper, revealing exactly what to say to your prospect on your sales call to get a yes instead of a no. In other words, this device reveals to you why they buy—the Holy Grail of sales!

To reveal the yes inside, you have to slide the discs into the perfect order of their B.A.N.K. code. Get one letter wrong, the yes remains elusive. Remember, this device is booby-trapped with a vial of vinegar. If you fail to crack the code correctly, you'll instead crack open the tiny vial of vinegar, dissolving the possibility of the sale and turning your potential yes into a no.

Have you ever experienced this moment in real life, where you felt your sale shift from a yes to a no? Not only did you go home empty-handed, but you lost a valuable treasure forever. Every one of your goals and dreams was locked inside that cryptex as well. Your ability to pay your bills, own your home, fund your kids' college education, travel to places on your bucket list, and achieve your dreams all dissolved in the vinegar, vaporizing right in front of your eyes! Ouch!

I have two questions for you now:

1. How often is this happening to you?
2. How much is it costing you?

Chances are, your failure to crack the code likely costs you hundreds of thousands of dollars per year and millions of dollars over your lifetime.

@CheriTree #WhyTheyBuy

Focusing on learning traditional sales techniques to close the sale will likely result in broken vials of vinegar and unmet sales goals—you still aren't focusing on the ultimate truth of sales: that *why they buy* is ultimately much more valuable than knowing how to sell. This could be the most expensive mistake you're making. If you don't crack this code, you'll likely lose much more than just money.

CHAPTER 8

THE OPPORTUNITY COST

"Let your prospect determine your presentation."

– Tony Robbins

In 1992, the Chally Group, now a Growth Play company, conducted a research project known as the World Class Sales project. Their research revealed that:

"Only 18% of buyers will buy from a salesperson who doesn't match the buyer's personality type verses 82% success when personality types are aligned."

– The Chally Group #WhyTheyBuy

Wow! When I read this, I was blown away! This information has been available for more than twenty-five years—how was it possible that more people weren't talking about this in every book or course on sales? This statistic validated everything I was experiencing, and it gave me the drive to follow my course and shout it from the rooftops!

In more recent years, a consulting company named Altify, together with Salesforce.com, revealed that an alarming 66 percent of customers are turned off by the sales presentation delivered by the person trying to sell to them.

These two statistics validate my theory and heavily stack the odds against the average salesperson. Without correcting this, you're likely heading straight into the sales maytag where you'll inevitably get more nos, and risk destroying your morale and self-esteem as well—all because you struggle to communicate effectively with your prospect.

What if there were a scientific way to say the right thing to your prospect every single time? Could the solution be as simple as following motivational speaker Tony Robbins' advice at the beginning of this chapter?

That quote was an eye-opener for me. Let my prospect determine my presentation? I could do that! If there are four personality types, then, technically, I should have four sales presentations, one for each type. Yet, every company I'd ever worked for had given me only one single presentation, and then asked me to deliver that presentation over and over and over, expecting to get more nos and calling it a numbers game! That was the recipe for failure.

THE GREATEST MISTAKE

No wonder 66 percent of customers say they're turned off by a salesperson who basically delivered the wrong presentation to them. This made sense to me now. Based on personality science, the greatest mistake I was making was delivering the wrong presentation to my prospective customer, or essentially, speaking the wrong language or code.

The theories of personality science helped me understand that there are essentially four different types of people in the world. Whichever personality type I am dominant in, I speak, communicate, and sell to my customer from that point of view.

This meant I was likely delivering the right presentation to one out of the four groups, and it also meant I was likely delivering the wrong presentation to the other three out of four.

This catastrophic mistake was likely resulting in me delivering the wrong sales presentation up to 75 percent of the time, leaving hundreds of thousands of dollars on the table!

@CheriTree #WhyTheyBuy

MY LOSSES FROM DELIVERING THE WRONG PRESENTATION

To add insult to injury, I also realized I was driving customers away from me and over to my competitors at a rate of three to one, because for every no I got, that customer was likely going over to my competition.

This one single mistake I was making was costing me a fortune...and I wanted to see the math for myself so I could determine my opportunity cost.

$ 72,000 (CURRENT INCOME) X 3 = $ 216,000 (EXTRA INCOME)

X 20 (NUMBER OF YEARS REMAINING IN SALES)

= $ 4,320,000.00 (MONEY YOU CAN TAKE TO THE BANK)

When I did this math, I realized my losses were literally costing me the difference between making it to the Wealthy 1 percent club (net worth of $5 million or more) and retiring broke like 95 percent of the people in our country!

Here's my math: My annual income at the time was $72,000. I multiplied it by 3, representing the 3 out of 4 groups to whom I was likely delivering the wrong presentation. That equaled a loss of $216,000 per year. Ouch! Remember, at the time I was $30,000 in credit card debt, renting an apartment, and driving a salvaged BMW. I really could have used that extra income, trust me!

Next, I multiplied my annual loss times the number of years I would likely still be working. I was ambitious at thirty, so I thought I'd give it another twenty years and work until I was fifty. $216,000 x 20 years = $4,320,000 in lost revenue. Double ouch! This was my opportunity cost, and it was killing me financially.

WHAT ARE YOU LOSING BY GIVING THE WRONG PRESENTATION?

Most salespeople don't calculate the true cost of a no. It's not just the loss of the revenue on that one sale, but it's also the loss of the lifetime value of the client and his or her entire referral network. This could be costing you untold millions in lost revenue over your career. For me, the opportunity cost was so massive that I had no choice but to try to crack the code and stop the bleeding.

Calculate the money you could be making every year simply by closing all the prospects who are likely to buy. Have you got the number? If you're still just guessing, it's not enough. Do the exercise at the end of this chapter and get the real figures. If you're like me, you'll likely be shocked at how much you're losing.

I have a question for you. Are you ready to take that money to *your bank* instead? If yes, then read on and find out how sales linguistics can be making or breaking each and every sale!

- Calculate your own losses. Fill in your numbers and see whether the opportunity cost of not learning this system is worth it.
- If you have a company with a sales team, multiply this number times the number of salespeople on your team. This figure may warrant a discussion with our company sooner, rather than later!

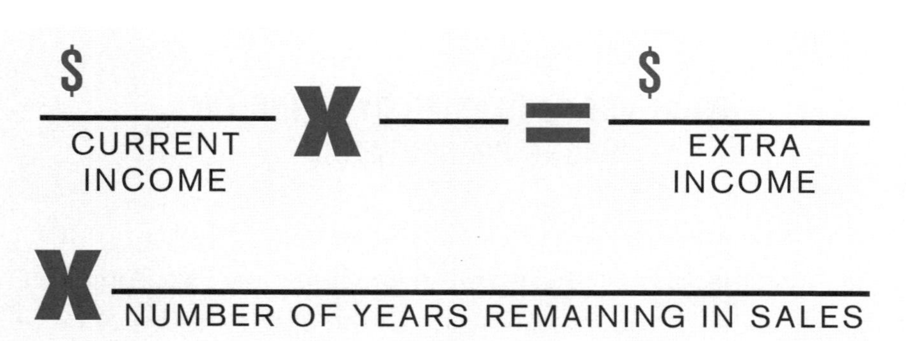

If your numbers above were five-figures or higher, we can help you stop the bleeding and recapture a much larger percentage of your lost revenue. Ideally, I'd personally like to consult with each of my customers and help them build out an entirely "BANKIFIED" sales and marketing strategy that gives them a significant competitive advantage. This type of service is not cheap, but the results I can deliver at that level are amazing. To put it in perspective, for that service, my company charges a retainer and percentage of sales, which combined adds up to one million dollars. I understand that many of my customers won't be able to pay me for that level of service, which is why I have developed the tools, training, and technology that are more affordable to the masses. This book is a great way to start to understand the B.A.N.K. system, but as you read, keep my offer in mind. A million dollars is nothing when the results my company can provide for you can lead to many more millions.

CHAPTER 9

SALES LINGUISTICS

"The single biggest problem in communication is the illusion that it has taken place."

– George Bernard Shaw

From the time I was a little girl, I absolutely loved learning different languages. Languages are a beautiful and essential part of the communication process. The words you say (and write) to others can create a lasting impression—either good or bad—and ultimately impact your success in sales and in life. Therefore, you've got to choose them wisely.

When you're communicating, whether on a formal sales call or in a casual conversation with a prospect, words matter. The right words can set the stage for a closer relationship, a huge closed deal, and a lasting, productive partnership. The wrong words can ruin all your careful efforts to build a productive relationship as fast as you can get the sentence out. The key to saying the right thing to anyone, especially your customer, is speaking the right language.

So how do you choose the right words? According to science, you can look to linguistics.

DEFINING LINGUISTICS

While most people hear linguistics and immediately think about exploring the mechanics of foreign languages, a comprehensive study of linguistics includes so much more. We can use linguistics to explore the impact our words have on the world.

Linguistics is the study of languages, from the nitty gritty rules of how we pronounce sounds and structure sentences to the more expansive ways that the meaning of language can change in context and even how our use of language influences the way others interpret a message. Linguists have long studied how word choice, tone, context, and thousands of other factors can influence the impact of a person's message.

Since sales is all about influence, it's no surprise that a whole discipline has emerged within linguistics to study the relationship between language and sales—*sales linguistics.* Sales linguistics is the scientific study of the language salespeople and prospects use during the sales process. Sales linguists focus on how the words they purposely choose speak to prospects' motives of why they buy, directly affecting their buying decisions. The language you use will significantly impact your likelihood of closing the sale.

When you study sales linguistics, you discover the power of language in influence. For me, discovering sales linguistics transformed the way I looked at all my interactions with prospects. But the power that language has in shaping our understanding of a message is something I first discovered many years ago.

BLAH, BLAH, BLAH, BONJOUR...

I had my first opportunity to learn a foreign language when I was five. My dad was a fighter pilot for the United States Air Force, and he was offered a special assignment to teach at the French Air Force Academy. This was an exciting opportunity for our entire family, so my parents accepted the assignment and moved our whole family to southern France for three years.

We moved during the summer, just before the school year was getting ready to start. My parents discussed what type of school I should attend, and they both agreed that putting me straight into a full immersion French-speaking school instead of sending me to an international English-speaking school would be a great opportunity. I'd experience the language in a way only kids really could and pick up French much faster.

When my first day of kindergarten (*maternelle*) arrived, my mom helped me pack my little backpack and sent me off for my very first school experience. With great anticipation, she waited for me to come home from this exciting day. She was particularly interested in finding out what I had learned. After all, I didn't speak a word of French.

As her little five-year-old daughter came home from school for the very first time, she sat me down and asked, "What did you learn today?"

My response was simple. I replied,

"Blah, blah, blah, bonjour!"

@CheriTree #WhyTheyBuy

My mom was caught a little off guard. She laughed and smiled! To be honest, she didn't exactly know what to expect! After all, I'd never learned French, and this was my first day going to school. It turns out that without the right language, most of the class was meaningless blather to me.

While the lessons in my kindergarten class may have been excellent for the French kids around me, they meant nothing to English-speaking me. I felt all kinds of emotions, from confusion and boredom to excitement and fear. It was hard to enjoy my education when I received it in the wrong language.

Of course, that was short-lived. I could still play with my classmates, even though I didn't speak their language. Within a short period of time, I became fluent in French and was speaking it like the local kids. Once I learned the language, my conversations with my teachers and other students suddenly had meaning. Attending French primary school ended up being a great experience. Once I knew the language, it wasn't just "blah, blah, blah" anymore.

SPEAKING THE RIGHT LANGUAGE WITH YOUR PROSPECTS

When you speak to a five-year-old in a foreign language on a daily basis, there's a great chance that five-year-old will simply dedicate herself to learning your language. Adults in business may not have the same reaction, especially if you only get one chance to meet someone and make a good impression. If I walked into a sales call here in the U.S. and only spoke in French, most prospects would just hear "Blah, blah, blah," and resolve not to have another meeting with the weird woman who insisted on speaking French, even though they couldn't understand her.

Now before you roll your eyes and close the book, I know you probably aren't going to make such a huge mistake as to speak the actual wrong official language in a sales call. Unfortunately, you may be using the wrong language regardless.

According to linguistics, the language you speak isn't just defined as English, French, or Chinese. Context matters. On some level, you already know this, even without studying the science of linguistics. After all, you probably use very different language at work from what you would use with your kids at home. Different situations require different tones, vocabulary, and levels of formality.

In fact, according to sales linguists, every single person actually speaks a completely unique language. We each have a totally one-of-a-kind outlook on life due to a unique combination of factors, including our personality, history, career, budget, financial status, culture, and much more. How different people talk about a product or business opportunity will change depending on an individual's language. Even the exact same words will be interpreted differently by individuals with dramatically different "personal languages."

You may think your sales script is saying one thing, but to someone who speaks another language, it may say something else entirely. That is why you risk turning off more prospects than you turn on and, ultimately, losing the sale.

BLAH, BLAH, BLAH, BUY MY PRODUCT!

When I was starting out as a professional salesperson, I had little luck making the sale using the suggested presentation script on clients. To increase my close rate, I spent hours perfecting my presentation. I took the standard, suggested script from my company and transformed it into what I thought would be the perfect lines to get the Yes. I felt so excited to finish my ideal sales script and use it on my prospects.

It turned out that my ideal script wasn't very effective, either. My close rate stayed frustratingly low. Something was wrong. In fact, no matter how much I improved my standard script, the close rate didn't budge much. After conferring with other people on my team, I realized that not a single script was consistently winning over prospects. While we each approached the sale differently and each closed a number of sales, no sales script was getting the message through 100 percent of the time.

That's when I realized that the problem wasn't with each script itself but with the idea that a single script could cover everyone's language. Something in the message wasn't connecting or resonating with prospects who said no. They couldn't understand a script in my language if their language wasn't like my own. I was inadvertently limiting my prospects to those who were most like me.

Today, I realize that every single time I delivered a sales presentation to a customer and got a no, I wasn't speaking that customer's language. It was the equivalent of me saying, "Blah, blah, blah, buy my product" or "Blah, blah, blah, join my team." The message wasn't getting through. It was all noise. Sometimes prospects would just stare back at me as if I were speaking a foreign language…and then it occurred to me—I was! If you are getting lots of nos, you may be making the exact same linguistic mistakes I made.

THE ROSETTA STONE

As a kid, I was willing to listen to a little "blah, blah, blah" in another language to connect with my classmates, but your prospect isn't going to be quite so willing to listen to you carrying on in the wrong language or code. Time is money, and your prospects will only attempt to translate your message into their own language for so long before moving on.

If you want your message to get through, you have to adapt your language so each prospect can understand it. When you just continue to use a single script, most of your clients will only hear "blah, blah, blah" as you are making an offer. When you fail to deliver your presentation in the language or code of your prospect, you are demonstrating either ignorance or arrogance. This will result in losing the prospect's attention, respect, and, ultimately, the sale.

To connect with others, expand your influence, and succeed in sales, you've got to learn to speak other people's languages and quickly adapt your own ways of communicating. This is essentially the essence of *Why They Buy*. For most people, this can feel intimidating, especially if you don't know what language to use.

Luckily, B.A.N.K. has a Rosetta Stone impact, using personality science as the essential clue to reveal a fast and easy way to speak your prospect's language in a fully systematic and charismatic way–making B.A.N.K. the universal language of people.

@CheriTree #WhyTheyBuy

“Everything must be made as simple as possible. But not simpler.”

— Albert Einstein

SECTION 3: THE SYSTEM

In Section 2, I revealed the missing link and taught you the science behind increasing your sales using personality science, buyology, and sales linguistics. Now it's time to apply that science and make it work to your advantage through the B.A.N.K. system.

When I was developing B.A.N.K., I collected all the characteristics related to buying decisions from as many different types in personality typing systems as I could find. I re-categorized them according to four distinct "buying personalities." Over time, clear behavior patterns emerged, and I was able to establish the key sales strategies that work best with each type. Independent studies that validated these types only proved what I knew all along: the B.A.N.K. personality typing system is a more effective way to communicate, negotiate, and sell to anyone because it reveals exactly *why they buy*.

The way it works is simple. Four basic categories of personality characteristics influence the way we make buying decisions. In the context of the B.A.N.K. system, I call these personality types **Blueprint**, **Action**, **Nurturing**, and **Knowledge**. Each person draws from all of them, but depending on your personality type, you lean toward certain ones more than others—and some may matter to you little or not at all.

Each buying personality has a set of shared values and typical behavior patterns that make that individual unique. These values and behaviors make the person more receptive to certain approaches and communication strategies and determine what decisions he or she is most likely to make. The values of each B.A.N.K. type similarly correspond to a number of adaptive selling behaviors that work best with each personality type.

In case you aren't familiar with them, adaptive selling behaviors (or ASBs, for short) are specific alterations in the way you communicate standard sales information (aka your "presentation") to empathize better with the unique situation of the person you are selling to. ASBs have long been shown to make sales presentations both more effective and more appealing to prospective clients. B.A.N.K. leverages many of these proven strategies, as well as newly discovered tactics, but the system also improves upon the old ASB model by simply clarifying which prospects prefer which selling behaviors—and thus what true empathy looks like for different types of people.

B.A.N.K. ensures that you can accurately type a prospect in the first ninety seconds of an encounter, rather than providing fuzzy categories that can only be defined through trial and error, or the antiquated "mirror and matching" advice. Your approach to sales in these outdated ASB models turns many prospects off before you even manage to choose the right selling behavior. It's time to embrace the cutting-edge science of the B.A.N.K. system for more yeses and a way out of the sales maytag.

In this section, I am going to delve deeper into the four personality types so you can learn the values of each, as well as the adaptive selling behaviors that help you communicate and sell better to each type. I'll include chapters that focus on how you can embrace your inner Blueprint, Action, Nurturing, and Knowledge type more closely no matter what your personal B.A.N.K. code is. When I learned to tap into each part of my code (even my weakest types), I was able to relate better to all the codes that differed from mine and dramatically improve my sales results.

Finally, I'll wrap up with a chapter that puts the whole system together so you can crack the entire B.A.N.K. code. You'll learn why a person's whole code affects the way you should interact with him or her for a better relationship—and skyrocketing sales! The B.A.N.K. system reveals the ultimate tactics for more wins, so you need to make mastering the B.A.N.K. codes a priority. I will outline the entire system and reveal the crux of *why they buy* in this section.

CHAPTER 10

BLUEPRINT

INSIDE THE BOX

"If you never venture outside the box, you will probably not be creative. But if you never get inside the box, you will certainly be stupid."

– Christopher Peterson

Our first B.A.N.K. code is Blueprint. I like to classify Blueprint types as "inside the box." For a Blueprint, his box is his comfort zone, so anything outside the box is risky. He typically doesn't venture outside the box, but focuses on staying inside it.

In the B.A.N.K. system, I associate each type with one of the primary colors. The color associated with Blueprint is blue. For one, the color blue is in the word Blueprint. This type is also a little colder when you interact with them, and the color blue is often associated with cold. Blueprints can sometimes come across as cold and firm. In addition, an architect's blueprints themselves are blue—and they are planned out carefully (just like everything a Blueprint type does).

UNDERSTANDING BLUEPRINT TYPES

In order to use the right selling behaviors with Blueprints, you need to understand their key values, motivations, likes, dislikes, and typical behaviors. This section digs deep into who Blueprints are so you can better speak their language.

KEY MOTIVE

The key motive for Blueprint types is to be safe and protect themselves from risk or danger.

@CheriTree #WhyTheyBuy

Therefore, Blueprints' core values are there to protect them. Their mantra is, "It's better to be safe than sorry." Therefore, anything that represents risk in any way will likely lose the sale.

VALUES

There are twelve core values for Blueprints. These are:

1. Stability
2. Structure
3. Systems
4. Planning
5. Processes
6. Predictability
7. Responsibility
8. Duty
9. Rules
10. Credentials
11. Titles
12. Tradition

Each value drives their decisions, and thus, their buying behavior. Let's review each of these values in more detail so you understand the meaning and significance behind each Blueprint value.

STABILITY

A Blueprint type values stability. If you think of the architect who designed your home, that person valued stability. He or she wanted to build everything on a very solid foundation. The same is true in business. That means the stability of your company, the stability of your product line, the stability of your pricing model, or perhaps even the stability of you as the salesperson or representative of that product, service, or opportunity needs to be built on a firm foundation. You see, if you come across as unstable, or the company or the product does, Blueprint types are not going to do business with you because stability is a primary value for this type, and the lack of it is risky.

STRUCTURE

Consequently, there has to be a structure to everything. Whether you're talking about the company structure, the management team's organizational structure, the pricing structure, or your personal business operation and infrastructure, Blueprints value and need structure in order to avoid risk. Look at the way you're presenting your information and make sure you're highlighting a very solid structure.

SYSTEMS

SYSTEM as an acronym stands for Save Your Self Time, Energy, and Money. Blueprints love systems because they're effective, productive, and predictable. A system gives predictable results. Blueprints love to follow systems. Start looking in your presentation where you can focus on systems and walking your prospect through a very sequential process. That's why the franchise model has been so successful as a business model. After all, nine out of ten traditional businesses fail. In network marketing, less than 10 percent of salespeople make more than $10 a week. However, because franchises use a system, more than 80 percent of them succeed. That's a huge swing from failure to success. Why? Because that business model is built on very predictable, cookie-cutter, proven systems—which reduces risk.

PLANNING

Blueprint types love to plan everything, from their scheduled appointments and budgets to their grocery lists and vacation packing lists. As Benjamin Franklin once said, "If you fail to plan, you plan to fail!" Lack of planning significantly increases risk, cost, loss of time, etc. As a result, everything must be planned. If it's not planned, it likely won't happen. If you poorly manage your time or demonstrate a lack of planning ahead, you'll likely lose the sale. According to a Blueprint, if you're on time, you're late, and if you're early, you're on time. Blueprints plan to arrive at their appointments fifteen to thirty minutes early. As I mentioned in Chapter 1, I lost a deal by being late ten minutes. I didn't plan my arrival time well enough, and it cost me thousands of dollars in lost commissions.

Yikes! That was a really valuable learning lesson. I made sure I never repeated that mistake again; if there was even a chance I was going to be late, I called ahead to notify my prospect. Planning ahead is really important. If you're going to have an appointment with a Blueprint, you can't just swing by spontaneously and expect that person to drop everything in his schedule that he's been planning for weeks or sometimes months. You actually have to request an appointment and do it a week or two out to get on his books if you really want him to pay solid attention to what you have to say. Respect that about Blueprints and you'll close more sales.

PROCESSES

Blueprint types love processes because a process reduces risk. A process is a series of actions or steps taken to achieve a particular end. Stephen Covey revealed Habit #2 in his book *The 7 Habits of Highly Effective People*: "Begin with the end in mind." This means that you need to understand all of your processes because a Blueprint wants to know what the end is, and then wants to know all the steps to get from the beginning to the end. When you master this value, you will be able to take your Blueprint clients through a step-by-step process from A to Z, from 1 through 10, literally showing them their exact moves and every milestone, step by step. If it's a process, they can follow it and, thus, reduce risk. A process is predictable, which leads us to the next value.

PREDICTABILITY

Blueprints crave predictability because it eliminates the fear of the unknown. The ability to predict the future, forecast sales, anticipate their competitors' actions in the marketplace, or even predict the amount of money they are spending or earning is key to survival for Blueprints. They absolutely do not like risk, and they do everything they can to avoid it. Again, in Chapter 1, I shared the story of losing a large deal by simply being ten minutes late to my appointment. My client was predicting that I would likely drop other balls in the future, and, therefore, he could predict a track record of disappointments that was too risky to assume, so he terminated the deal.

RESPONSIBILITY

Responsibility implies that you are accountable for something and that you take ownership of that fact. With Blueprints, you must prove that you are responsible and reliable. Your word is your bond. A handshake means you have a deal and you must follow through with every commitment. You show up early to appointments. You adhere to their budget requirements. You follow up with them regularly. You never drop balls. Essentially, you are able to demonstrate that you can be trusted, which is very important to Blueprints because it reduces risk.

DUTY

A duty is a moral or legal obligation, and it comes from the word "due," meaning "that which is owing." A duty comes with an expectation. Blueprint types expect you to keep your word, adhere to the contract, follow the policy, stay within budget, show up on time, etc. Often, a Blueprint will not be flexible or bend the rules for you. So to win business with your Blueprint prospects, you must exemplify a 100 percent commitment to every agreement, written or spoken.

RULES

Fill in the blank: Rules were meant to be ____________. If you said "broken," you are not a Blueprint! According to the Blueprints, rules were meant to be followed, and they expect everyone to follow the rules. Without rules, processes would fail, people could die, economies and governments might even collapse. Rules are not suggestions—rules are rules, and Blueprints expect you to follow them! If you don't follow them, they are more than happy to enforce them. Don't believe me? Try speeding and watch what happens when you get pulled over by local law enforcement! If the police officer is a Blueprint, I can guarantee you that you will get a ticket, no matter how much you cry or bat your eyelashes! Blueprints can be very disciplinary in the way they interact. For example, a rule with my client whom I was meeting with was, "Don't be late." Unfortunately, he never told me that in advance. I found out the hard way. I was late. I broke his rule. I paid the penalty—I lost that sale.

CREDENTIALS

A credential implies that you have a qualification for something in particular, and it is often used in reference to your personal background or work history to indicate that you are suitable or capable of meeting certain requirements. Thus, if you have a credential like a master's degree, you are assumed to be more qualified for the job, which reduces the risk of selecting someone less qualified. Corporations around the world place a lot of emphasis on a person's credentials, and so do your Blueprint prospects. If someone hands you her business card and it has the acronym M.B.A. after her name, that person is likely a Blueprint. Other M.B.A. graduates may not put that credential on their business cards because it's not as important to them as it is for Blueprints.

TITLES

A title can be used to convey respect based on nobility, academic degree, important accomplishments, or more commonly, to reflect the office or position of an official or executive in an organization. Blueprints love titles because they respect authority and adhere to a specific pecking order in companies or even in society. A title gives a person credibility for his or her respective position, and for a Blueprint, it creates a level of implied respect based on their rank. Think of the military. There's a reason it has ranks. There's a reason there are certain behaviors expected from enlisted versus officers and a protocol for how they treat each other and greet each other, determined by who has more authority, etc. Be sure to put a legitimate title on your business card and make sure you acknowledge the title of your prospective client as well.

TRADITION

A tradition is the transmission of customs or beliefs that are passed on from generation to generation. Sometimes traditions lack logic or even relevance, but when a Blueprint is asked why he continues to do it, he will simply reply, "Because that's the way it's always been done." Put simply, Blueprints don't like change. Change equals risk, so they're far more likely to keep doing business with their current supplier, trainer, insurance person, etc. rather than switching to you. The key to getting them to break their tradition and switch their business over to you is to establish the fact that staying where they're at is riskier than moving their business to you.

OCCUPATIONS

Blueprints tend to work in jobs based on their core values. Some of these occupations might be accountants, teachers, lawyers, managers, and police or military officers. They seek out jobs that provide a fair amount of stability, structure, and so forth, where they can follow and even enforce rules, policy, legislation, budgets, compliance, and laws.

GREETING

Because Blueprints are fairly conservative, formal, and inside the box, they're likely to greet you with the customary greeting of your culture. For example, in the U.S., the typical greeting is a handshake and a, "Nice to meet you." In Europe, it is two or three kisses on the cheek. In Asia, it is often a bow. The key is to pay attention to the customary greeting and follow suit.

CLUES

One way to recognize a Blueprint is to look for a particular set of clues, listed here.

- Professional Dress
- Conservative
- Organized
- Punctual
- Formal
- Clean
- Articulate
- Polite and Respectful
- Credentialed
- Thrifty
- On a Budget
- Drives Economical Cars with High Safety Ratings

LIKES

After surveying thousands of Blueprints, I have created lists of their top likes and dislikes. This list of likes can help you identify the things they want or need as part of their buying language.

- Accountability
- Budgets
- Commitment
- Consistency
- Directions
- Discipline
- Discounts
- Due Diligence
- Goals
- Guarantees
- Insurance
- Integrity
- Lists
- Loyalty
- Order
- Organizing
- Perfection
- Proven Plans
- Punctuality
- References
- Routines
- Savings
- Sequential Steps
- Track Records

DISLIKES

Just as the list above reveals the top items that Blueprints like, this list reveals their dislikes. You should avoid these in your sales and communication process.

- Blame
- Carelessness
- Change
- Chaos
- Clutter
- Danger
- Debt
- Delays
- Disorder
- Exaggeration

- Instability
- Interruptions
- Irresponsibility
- Jokes
- Missing Deadlines
- Overspending
- Paying Interest
- Risk
- Rule Breakers
- Surprises
- Tardiness
- Unclear Instructions
- Unreliability
- Waste

SUMMING UP THE BLUEPRINT PERSONALITY

As you can see, Blueprints are some of the most fair and dependable people around. They believe in following the rules. Blueprints value getting the details and logistics right—they dot the i's and cross the t's. They believe in finding every way possible to reduce risk and follow proven, time-tested systems that deliver results. When you remember Blueprints' core personality and motivation, you'll understand *why they buy*.

BLUEPRINT ASBS

Of course, just knowing what Blueprints are like doesn't necessarily give you a roadmap for how to close a sale with them. Luckily, specific adaptive selling behaviors (ASBs) have been proven to increase the likelihood of a successful sale with Blueprints. Following are some buying triggers and sales tips you can use to get the yes from Blueprints.

BUYING TRIGGERS

Independent research studies analyzed the top buying triggers (actions, facts, or realities established during the buying process that trigger a yes) for each code. Here are the Top Five Buying Triggers for those whose dominant code is Blueprint:

1. Staying within their budget.
2. Excellent written details describing the product or service.
3. Positive overall reputation of the company or person they're buying from.
4. Positive recommendations from people they know.
5. Positive overall product/service ratings from customers.

SALES TIPS

Using the right buying triggers alone isn't enough, though. Now that you understand more about Blueprint types, you've got to use the right ASBs in every step of the sales process to close the sale. Following are key sales tips and strategies I want to recommend to you. Each of these selling behaviors will help you build better rapport, speak Blueprints' language, and increase the chance of closing your sale.

- Be professional, organized, and on time.
- Have a step-by-step plan you can give them.
- Don't be too pushy or exaggerate.
- Stay within budget.
- Have your facts straight and resources in place so you can show proof to back your claim.
- Show them the system for success.
- Minimize the risk to get involved.

EMBRACING YOUR INNER BLUEPRINT

Now that you understand who Blueprints are and how to sell to them successfully, it's time to leverage your own inner Blueprint to drive more sales. I'm going to share some amazing success stories from my own life and a couple from my B.A.N.K. clients to show you how leveraging the Blueprint code can massively increase your sales success. Then, I'll summarize everything you've learned about Blueprints with some final strategies for closing sales with Blueprints.

SUCCESS STORY - JEFF V.

Here's the success story of my client Jeff Vogan. Jeff is a very successful financial advisor from Arizona. He was making several hundred thousand dollars a year, even prior to studying the B.A.N.K. program.

At first, Jeff was skeptical about the B.A.N.K. training. He didn't believe he could get a 300 percent increase in his sales closings, and he felt he was already making good money because he was pretty well-trained in sales. However, he realized that the opportunity cost of not investing in our training and attending our course was probably more expensive than not learning it, so he made the decision to invest in B.A.N.K. That was a very smart decision. Jeff applied himself and studied our program intensely to ensure he would get enough out of it to guarantee at least some return on his investment.

Meanwhile, one of his existing clients referred Jeff to his son, who was getting ready to retire and might need some help. The son was someone who did not do business with Jeff or his financial firm. When Jeff followed up with his client's son as he promised he would, the son immediately set his expectations upfront by telling Jeff, "Just so you know, I've agreed to take the appointment because my father recommended it. However, in the spirit of full disclosure, I don't plan to do business with you. I'm happy where I'm at, and I don't plan to move any of my money. I am, however, still happy to meet if you'd like, but it will likely be a waste of your time." Jeff, of course, chose to meet with him as a favor to his already existing client.

On the day of the appointment, Jeff got a text message from the guy twenty minutes prior to the appointment, stating that he'd already arrived at the restaurant. Only Blueprints arrive twenty minutes early! Jeff is an Action, not a Blueprint, which means he hoped to arrive as close to on time as possible. He had not even left his office building yet to go meet with this prospect. Jeff realized, *This is a clue. I'm studying B.A.N.K. and I just learned who arrives early—the Blueprint personality type.* Jeff left immediately to make sure he would arrive as early as possible. On the way to the appointment, he listened to my audio program for Blueprints. On it, he got advice for exactly what to do. He was coached through the process of how to sell to his Blueprint prospect.

Jeff met with his prospect. He delivered a sales presentation based on reducing risk, creating stability, and focusing on guarantees that were lacking in the prospect's current investment portfolio. He was completely professional with his prospect and focused on identifying the risks of where the prospect currently invested his money. He showed him a safer and more conservative approach that he would take if it were his money. At the end of the forty-minute appointment, the prospect looked at Jeff and said, "You know what? I had no intentions of moving my money to you, but I can clearly see now that it is the best decision. I would actually like to move my entire financial portfolio to you and your firm today. Do you have enough time to do that now, or do I need another appointment?" Obviously Jeff obliged that minute and produced the paperwork. (Of course! Jeff is an "A.")

Jeff was amazed by how much easier that meeting went than he had expected. *Wow! B.A.N.K. actually works*, he thought, and it was only his very first attempt at applying a true B.A.N.K. style sales approach. One simple clue about the prospect's B.A.N.K. code—that the client was at the appointment twenty minutes early—resulted in a major sale. As a matter of fact, Jeff went on to improve his income and cash flow by more than $50,000 in the next ninety days using the B.A.N.K. system. He was so impressed with what he had learned and how it had helped him communicate better with all types of clients and prospects that Jeff decided to train others in B.A.N.K., and he has helped many increase their revenues as well. Over the next twelve months, Jeff more than doubled his revenues and more than tripled his net income. He has never looked back and continues to improve sales year after year.

HOW I USED MY BLUEPRINT SIDE FOR SUCCESS

Jeff is not the only one who used his inner Blueprint for major business success. Blueprints love effective systems. Blueprint is the last part of my B.A.N.K. code, so I really had to get connected with that part of me to succeed in my business. Many times, I'd show up to an appointment without the proper documents, or I'd get back to my office only to discover I was missing signatures on the paperwork. Ugh! My lack of Blueprint was starting to cost me a lot of time and money, so I committed to getting this part of me reined in.

I got completely organized and developed a system for everything! I remember when I was selling life insurance, before I would even show up to my client's home to complete the application, I made sure I had every form for insurance, investments, mortgages, or whatever I was doing pre-filled out with as much data as possible. I went to the extent of actually organizing all of my client files according to color code. Every single client had a B.A.N.K. code, and I was sure to document it.

I created a client intake form that every client received with his or her entire four-digit B.A.N.K. code designated on the form with four colored sticker dots. This was important because each time I spoke with a client, I wanted to remind myself what his or her code was so I could adjust what I was saying or how I asked for referrals. Or if a new product came out, how I was going to get another appointment with my customer so he or she would consider doing perpetual business with me. I had each of my files color-coordinated based on the products I sold.

For example, my life insurance files were blue. I chose blue because the blood in your veins, as long as it stays in your veins, looks blue. My debt folders were red because when you're in debt, you're in the red. My investment portfolio folders were green because green represents money. My legal folders were yellow because estate planning was all about preserving the gold, and my agent folders were purple because purple represents royalty. People who worked with me were royalty in my eyes.

Every piece of business had its respective color code, and when I showed up to the customer's home, I would have everything already presorted and organized in each respective folder. I would have the right marketing materials, the right order forms, the right color codes for everything. As I laid out my files onto the customer's table or in my office, everything had an order, a process, and a system. Let me tell you, my clients' respect for me went through the roof when they saw how organized I was. Furthermore, because my credibility was so high, I was now able to do a lot more business.

Keep in mind, I became a financial advisor in my mid-twenties. I had absolutely no financial credibility whatsoever! After months of studying, I was able to pass my insurance and securities exams and started giving people financial advice. Ironically, I didn't own a home and didn't have a mortgage. I didn't have any money and, therefore, I didn't have my own investment portfolio. And I didn't even have a family so there was no need for an insurance policy of my own. Why in the world would anyone take financial advice from me?

Well, it happened to be a career that I really liked. Ever since I was a kid with my own candy business, I liked talking about money. I liked talking about the stock market and investment portfolios, and because it was a career path I liked, I knew I had to get an enormous head start and create credibility through organization and professionalism if I was going to win my Blueprint clients' business. I treated it so seriously. I made sure I did all of my continuing education and that I became a well-read professional.

As a result, I wrote a lot more business and rose to the top of that organization. I became a Regional Vice President with one of the largest financial services companies in the country. I began running my own location. I had an entire office full of agents whom I led. I got my securities principals license so I could oversee the financial transactions happening in my sales organization.

So even though I might be a top-of-the scale Action type, the truth is my understanding of the Blueprints was something really critical for my financial success in business. Therefore, I encourage you, if you're going to do any business with the Blueprints, adhere to their values and follow my guidelines. They work!

BLUEPRINT SUMMARY

Let's summarize the Blueprint type. In general, out of the four classifications of personality types, Blueprints are the ones who are predictable to a T.

When you understand the human nature of a Blueprint, you'll know to deliver your sales presentation in a way that's cool, calm, and collected, fact-driven, black and white, processed and systematic.

Be prepared going into the presentation. Be on time. Be responsible. Call ahead to schedule appointments. Have processes for filling out your paperwork and submitting contracts.

Do the things I'm suggesting and I promise your Blueprint clients will like you, trust you, and respect you more. They'll feel safe doing business with you. They will know that if you give them a handshake or a promise, that your word is bankable. If you are a Blueprint and you're doing business with another Blueprint, then, of course, you're already a natural match. If you're not, remember to follow my advice.

Blueprints have a dress code, and they expect you to follow it. If you don't know it, find out. Don't show up looking like a beach bum if you're getting ready to meet with a Blueprint executive. You always need to match the Blueprints' dress code at their level or one level above so they respect you. If you do, then you're going to do a lot more business with them.

Last but not least, make sure you stay within your Blueprints' budget. Never, ever, ever go over budget! As a matter of fact, it's best if you're able to come in at least 10 percent under budget. This shows that you have a high regard for their money and you're doing your best to help them control their expenses. If they don't have the budget for your products or services, find a way to help them cut something else out of their budget or increase their topline revenue so they can afford more. Play it safe and close the deal!

EXERCISE

Memorize the twelve Blueprint values and become fluent in the Blueprint language.

Identify five things you can do so you can more effectively communicate, negotiate, and close more sales with a Blueprint:

1. ____
____
____
____

2. ____
____
____
____

3. ____
____
____
____

4. ____
____
____
____

5. ____
____
____
____

CHAPTER 11

ACTION

OUTSIDE THE BOX

"Don't think outside the box. Think like there is no box."

– Author Unknown

Our second B.A.N.K. code is Action. I like to classify Action types as outside the box. The box is way too confining for them, so they typically want nothing to do with it. In some cases, you'll even hear an Action type say, "What box?" and ignore it completely. Avoid anything to do with a box.

The color associated with Action is red. Action types are red hot, on fire, and act like they just drank Red Bull for breakfast! They're the movers, shakers, and millionaire-makers. They talk fast, drive fast, and live life on the red line. And they love to be treated like VIP celebrities so they like to receive red carpet treatment!

UNDERSTANDING ACTION TYPES

In order to use the right selling behaviors with Action types, you need to understand their key motives, values, motivations, likes, dislikes, and typical behaviors. This section digs deep into who Action types are so you can better speak their language.

KEY MOTIVE

> **The key motive for the Action type is to be the best! Failure is never an option for them.**
>
> **@CheriTree #WhyTheyBuy**

Therefore, their core values are there to help them win and enjoy a lifestyle that most people dream about. Their mantra matches the champion's creed of Muhammed Ali, the world's greatest boxer. When asked whether he liked training, he replied: "I hated every minute of training! But I said, 'Don't Quit. Suffer now—and live the rest of your life as a

Champion!'" Find a way to help your prospect be a champion and you'll definitely close the sale!

VALUES

There are twelve core values for Action:

1. Freedom
2. Flexibility
3. Spontaneity
4. Action
5. Opportunity
6. Excitement
7. Attention
8. Stimulation
9. Competition
10. Winning
11. Fun
12. Image

Each value drives Action types' decisions, and thus, their buying behavior. Let's review each value in more detail so you understand the meaning and significance behind it.

FREEDOM

Action types want to experience the essence of freedom in every way, including financial freedom, the freedom to be their own bosses, and the freedom to live their lives on their own terms. They never want to be told where to be, when to show up, how much they can spend, or what they should do. They want to be in full control of their destinies and be the captains of their ships. Only they can decide what's best for them, so make sure you don't back them into corners or put them in boxes. With Action types, it's usually "their way or the highway."

FLEXIBILITY

Action types are always looking for the best option, and they value flexibility so they can change their minds at any time. If a better option presents itself, they want to feel free to choose that instead. A one-size-fits-all solution won't typically work for the Actions. Be sure to show them all the bells and whistles, and find a plan they can change, start, or stop at any time. When it comes to pricing, give them two or three options and allow them to choose the plan that works best for them. Be sure to highlight your top package and why it's the best choice, and then allow them to make their own choices without feeling boxed in.

SPONTANEITY

Nothing's more exciting for an Action than to do completely unpredictable, spontaneous things. You can call one up last minute and say, "Hey, buddy, listen; I got tickets to a concert with backstage passes! We need to be there in thirty minutes. I'm swinging by your house. Hop in my car, and we'll be off to have the experience of a lifetime!" The Action will literally drop everything, and I mean everything: an appointment with his or her spouse, or the kids' soccer game, or even possibly a client. Don't underestimate what Actions will do to live that spontaneous lifestyle. Find ways to be spontaneous with them, even if that simply means calling them the same day to invite them to lunch! Chances are, if you're fun and take them to a nice place, they'll join you!

ACTION

Although action is the name of the entire personality type category, it's also a very important value to them. It's so important that I will classify this value as massive action. Action types don't need to know everything or even have a plan before they get started! They live by Nike's creed—Just do it! Actions are called the movers, shakers, and millionaire-makers for a reason—because they make things happen! Part of their strategy might be just to throw a whole bunch of spaghetti noodles against that wall to see what sticks. But they do it fast enough and frequently enough that they can earn a lot of revenue because of that behavior. That might be offensive to some of the other four personality types, but this is their style, and it works for them. Typically, you can find Actions classified among the top producers of any sales organization, not because they're the most organized, the best at planning, the most calculating, or even the best educated, but simply because they take massive action.

OPPORTUNITY

Action types not only live for opportunity—they die for it! Whether it's discovering a new land like Christopher Columbus did, moving west for the California Gold Rush, or launching a new start up, Actions are willing to risk it all in exchange for the right opportunity. By definition, an entrepreneur is someone who is willing to assume risk in exchange for gain. That is why Action types prefer to start their own businesses. If you tell them that you have an incredible opportunity, they will come running. Conversely, if you tell Blueprints that you have an amazing opportunity, they will typically run away. Why? Because an opportunity to a Blueprint sounds like risk. An opportunity to an Action sounds like excitement, adrenaline, and something that could create unlimited possibilities. Be very careful about the way you talk about the word "opportunity" and make sure you're focusing on that single word specifically with your Action clients.

EXCITEMENT

Action types live for excitement! You can put in another "A" word here called "adrenaline." Anything that's exciting means it's not boring. Think about the action sports that the A types are attracted to. They're not attracted to generally slow-moving or passive sports like golf or tennis, unless they're playing in a tournament. The A types are going to be attracted to adrenaline-extreme sports, like snowboarding, heli-skiing, wakeboarding, surfing, racing, and more. They take the ultimate risks. They love skydiving, bungee-jumping, whitewater rafting—anything that gives them the thrill of being alive, or possibly even on the verge of death without crossing over that border. This means that you need to be pumped up about your products and your life when you meet with them. If that's a struggle, listen to loud music and drink a Red Bull on the way to your appointment!

ATTENTION

Action types are all about attention, as long as they are the center of it! It's all about me, me, me. I'll never forget one of my favorite lines from the movie *Beaches* with Bette Midler. Bette's character is hanging out with her best friend who is more of a Nurturing/Blueprint type. Bette's character is a total Action type. She's talking non-stop about herself. Then she says, "Enough about me. Let's talk about you. What do you think of me?" That's such a typical Action!

When you're meeting with that Action client, understand that everything you do should be to shine the spotlight on him. When you get laser-focused on making him the star of the show, then you're going to make a lot more dough!

STIMULATION

Action types require stimulation. You've heard of people with ADD (attention-deficit disorder). Let me tell you, ADD starts with an "A." Action types simply get bored when things aren't exciting. That's just a matter of fact, so find ways to spice things up! Take Actions to environments that are stimulating to them—stimulating to their eyes, their ears, or their entire psyche—places that have a lot of high energy, great music, or people buzzing around. Actions like to be around other people's energy. If you take them to a quiet, closed, sterile environment, you will likely bore them and lose the sale.

COMPETITION

Action types love competition! Competition is one of those things where losing is never an option. It's not negotiable. Actions compete to win. Notice how many A type personalities get attracted to sports or sales. Why? Because they don't want to have a boring job. Action types want the thrill of the hunt. They want to compete, and they compete to win.

I'll never forget watching the inauguration of Michael Jordan, the world's best basketball player, into the Basketball Hall of Fame. Millions of people were watching this epic moment in his career. He got up to the podium and said, "There's no I in team." I remember thinking to myself, "Wow, that was a really Nurturing thing to say." Then he said, immediately following that, "But there's an I in win," with a really big grin on his face. Find a way your clients can compete for the most referrals or largest deals, or even spotlight them as Client of the Month.

WINNING

Action types compete to win—and winning is not negotiable! In the movie *Talladega Nights*, about racing fast cars and winning, there's a line that says, "If you're not in first place, you're technically the first loser." That's exactly how Actions feel about winning and losing. Actions play to win in everything, from sports to business—they need to be the best. Losing is never an option, so find a way you can allow your prospect to win a negotiation with you, without you losing either. It could be a discount on price or even a limited-time bonus.

FUN

I have a saying: "If it's not fun, it's work—and I don't like to work!" Actions just want to have fun. They want to play games, laugh at jokes, go to concerts, play sports, travel the world, eat good food, listen to music, drive their convertibles, and live life in the fast lane! All work and no play makes for a very boring experience. Find ways to have fun with your clients. Take them to sporting events, nice restaurants, movie premieres, go-cart racing, music concerts, or even a barbeque at your home—anywhere they can have a good time.

IMAGE

Action types absolutely care about their images, and yours too! Their images reflect their reputations and what the outer world thinks of them. Action types care about making a good impression in the world, and they want the world to know they're the best. Action types live life as if they are on stage, and you are their audience. From head to toe, it's all for show.

When it comes to image, the Actions want the very best. Designer labels, the most expensive brands, or the most exclusive items you can buy are what the Action type gets excited about. Who do you think markets to these people? Ever heard of companies like Tiffany and Company, Robb Report, Mercedes, Ferrari, BMW, Bentley, Lamborghini? How about real estate companies like Sotheby's, five-star steakhouses like Ruth's Chris, and even writing instruments like Mont Blanc? These companies target Action clients who want to be in a league of their own, and are willing to pay to be the best or have the best.

OCCUPATIONS

Action types look for careers or businesses based on their core values. They may be actors, athletes, salespeople, public speakers, or entrepreneurs. They'll choose any type of occupation that will give them the freedom and flexibility to do things their way and the opportunity to earn unlimited income and live the dream.

GREETING

Because Action types are enthusiastic and outside the box, they need something far more stimulating than a handshake. Instead, they're likely to greet you with a high-five or a fist bump. They tend to be more animated and loud in a crowd.

CLUES

One way to recognize an Action is to look for a particular set of clues, listed here.

- Dressed to impress
- Designer Labels
- Bling/Flash/Cash
- Fashionably Late
- Animated
- Loud
- Fast
- Attention-seeking
- Energetic
- Great Hygiene
- Drive Expensive Cars
- Love Exclusivity
- Memberships
- VIP Treatment
- Celebrity Name Dropping
- Unorganized (unless to impress)

LIKES

After surveying thousands of Action types, I created a list of their top likes and dislikes. This list of likes can help you identify the things they want or need as part of their buying language.

- Beauty
- Bottom Line
- Celebrity Endorsements
- Confidence
- Credit
- Designer Brands
- Entertainment
- Expensive Cars
- Fame
- Fashion
- Fortune
- Games
- Glamour
- Incentives
- Luxuries
- Parties
- Power
- Prizes
- Recognition
- Results
- Speed
- Travel
- Variety
- VIP Treatment

DISLIKES

Just as the list above reveals the top items the Action types like, this list reveals the dislikes you should avoid in your sales and communication process.

- Boredom
- Bosses
- Boundaries
- Budgets
- Curfews
- Details
- Instructions
- Jobs
- Limits
- Losing
- Paperwork
- Planning
- Punctuality
- Repetition
- Routines
- Rules
- Saving
- Schedules
- Silence
- Speeding Tickets
- Tattle Tales
- Time Clocks
- Unnecessary Meetings
- Waiting

SUMMING UP THE ACTION PERSONALITY

As you can see, Action types are some of the most fun and independent people around. They are unafraid to take risks and are always on the lookout for new opportunities to disrupt and improve upon the status quo. If anyone is going to be involved in the next big thing, it's them! As big go-getters, Action types are always searching for better opportunities to be the best or have the best. When you remember Actions' core personality and motivation, you'll understand *why they buy*.

ACTION ASBS

Of course, just knowing what Action types are like doesn't necessarily give you a roadmap for how to close a sale with them. Luckily, specific adaptive selling behaviors are proven to increase the likelihood of a successful sale with A types. The following are some buying triggers and sales tips you can use to get the yes from Action types.

BUYING TRIGGERS

Our independent research studies analyzed the top buying triggers (actions, facts, or realities established during the buying process that trigger a yes) for each code. Here are the Top Five Buying Triggers for those whose dominant code is Action:

1. Celebrity endorsements
2. Media/social buzz

3. Automated recommendations (for example, "You purchased X, so you may be interested in Y.")
4. Reviews in relevant publications
5. Their gut feeling (instincts)

SALES TIPS

Using the right buying triggers alone isn't enough, though. Now that you understand more about Action types, you've got to use the right ASBs in every step of the sales process to close the sale. These are key sales tips and strategies I want to recommend to you. Each of these selling behaviors will help you build better rapport with Action types, speak their language, and increase the chance of closing the sale.

- Be cool and dress to impress.
- Display excitement and enthusiasm.
- Skip small talk; get straight to the bottom line.
- Have a sense of urgency.
- Sell the sizzle, lifestyle, and dream.
- Don't overload with details, charts, and information.
- Introduce them to other successful "A" personalities.

EMBRACING YOUR INNER ACTION

Now that you understand who Action types are and how to sell to them successfully, it's time to leverage your own inner Action to drive more sales. I'm going to share some amazing success stories from my own life and from other awesome B.A.N.K. clients to show you how leveraging the Action code can massively increase your sales success. Then,

I'll summarize everything you've learned about Action types with some final strategies for closing sales with them.

SUCCESS STORY - ESTHER W.

Here's a success story about Esther Wildenberg, a business consultant and entrepreneur from the Netherlands. In 2013, Esther attended a large conference in Amsterdam with more than 5,000 people in attendance. She was there to see Robert Kiyosaki and Les Brown.

As fate would have it, I happened to be speaking at this event as well. This was my first time speaking about B.A.N.K. in Europe, and I announced during my speech that I was looking for trainers and leaders who wanted to help me expand B.A.N.K. into Europe. Before I was even done talking, Esther had already made her way to my sales booth and bought my program! Actions don't wait for things to happen—they make them happen.

Over the conference's next couple of days, Esther continually visited our sales booth to connect with me and my business partner. Knowing this was my first time in Amsterdam, Esther and her business partner, Truus Druyts, invited us to dinner and showed us a good time. Actions like to create a wine-and-dine experience with their clients, and this was no exception. She created the opportunity to talk about the expansion of B.A.N.K. into Europe and how she could help.

Once Esther attended our B.A.N.K. course in Amsterdam a week later, she chose to become officially certified as one of our first B.A.N.K. trainers in Europe. She asked me when I was leaving the country, and whether I would be willing to help her do her first presentation if she organized a group. I said I would be happy to help, but I was leaving in four days and I needed a minimum of fifty people in attendance.

With no time to waste, Esther immediately went into massive action and organized a group of fifty-four people to attend a B.A.N.K. presentation in a bed and breakfast in Belgium, three hours away. She organized my transportation and made it all happen. At her launch event, she sold more than $40,000 worth of our product. Within the next few months, Esther and her business partner had become the top salespeople in our company.

Esther was the Action leader we were looking for to help us expand into Europe. She was the type who put her money where her mouth was and made things happen. Within six months, she had sold more than a half-million dollars of our B.A.N.K. training products and helped us expand into five countries. Her sales track record and outstanding leadership earned her a position with our company as the first International Sales Director.

As you may have heard, the pace of the leader is the pace of the pack. Esther led by example, and she not only helped us to establish the market in Europe, but she then began to assist with our global expansion into Asia, Africa, and deeper into North America. Her leadership and willingness to demonstrate massive action allowed her to gain tremendous respect with her clients, her peers, and our corporate team. Esther was the first certified and licensed B.A.N.K. trainer to do more than one million dollars in sales revenue in our company, and today she works full-time for BANKCODE corporate as the Executive Vice President of Global Sales.

HOW I USED MY ACTION SIDE FOR SUCCESS

Action types like Esther get big things done fast! I have seen this firsthand. As a full-force Action, I also use my A side to build my success every day. I will share two personal stories to illustrate how I leveraged my inner A to drive more sales and live the dream.

In this first story, I found a home I really, really loved—but it was way more than I could comfortably afford. It was a $2,000,000 home and the most expensive property I'd ever purchased for myself up to that point. I had to put at least a six-figure down payment on it, but I wanted to buy as much home as I could possibly afford, even if it felt crazy to everyone else. I knew that living the dream meant that I would stay focused on growing my business and income. My plan was to find a way to leverage my own piece of property, my home, and turn it into an absolute lifestyle pad that would drive more sales.

It was the epitome of a home built for entertainment, with a 600-bottle wine cellar and cocktail bar, sweeping views of the Pacific Ocean, a modern gas fireplace with crystals, contemporary artwork on the walls, a saltwater fish tank, arcade games, a private elevator that took me to my master suite, and a rooftop deck with a top-of-the-line BBQ grill and private deck with sunbeds. In the morning I would eat my breakfast out on the deck as I watched the dolphins swimming by, and in the evening, I would stare out at the city lights along the coast under the heat lamps and just relax and take it all in. This was my version of living the dream!

In order to justify the purchase, I found a way to leverage my expense and turn it into an asset by entertaining my clients and sales teams there. I would throw client appreciation parties and invite my existing clients over to my home with a VIP invitation. The rule to attend my parties was you had to bring a guest with you—someone who was not a client of mine. This allowed me to be introduced to my clients' networks in a more exclusive way. I never did any business at my parties, but I built relationships with people who wanted to connect and do business with me shortly thereafter.

My parties were first class. I brought in private chefs to pass around hors d'oeuvres. I cranked up incredible music and created a fun club atmosphere. I hired bartenders to take drinks around to all of my customers. I even had my own ice sculpture made with the brand logo for my company out on the patio deck. My parties were off the charts, but that drove the sales results that more than paid for my home every single month, to where affording it was no longer even an issue.

Throwing client appreciation events that are first class is one way to do more business with the A's.

Let me share another Action story with you. It's a story where I took my income from $8,000 to $261,000 in 28 days. This story illustrates the point of *massive action.*

In 2006, I made a New Year's resolution to earn $1,000,000 that year. I had never done it before. It seemed impossible, but I've been programmed my entire life to go for my goals and never hold back. I read a motivational print once that said, "It's what we dream that sets us apart." I was that dreamer. To make this dream happen, I needed to average $83,333 per month, or $250,000 per quarter.

Unfortunately, the year was off to a bad start. By the end of January, I had only earned $8,000 in commissions—not even 10 percent of my monthly goal. That's when I realized, "Houston, we have a problem." In order for me to get on track for my million-dollar year, I needed to earn $158,666 the following month. Yikes! The amount felt so overwhelming and beyond my reach that I decided the only way to do it was just to do something crazy—really crazy!

Since failure is never an option and I am programmed to win, I decided I would make my goal so insane that I would go for the entire income goal for the quarter the very next month—$250,000! Even more challenging, the next month was February with only twenty-eight days. Double yikes!

No one even believed that this was possible. Many people told me I was crazy! Some even told me I would be a fool if I publicly announced this because I was sure to fail, and that would not look good for my reputation. I felt like Roger Bannister, the first man to break the four-minute mile. No one believed that was possible either. I knew there was only one way to hit it—by taking massive action like I'd never done before!

For the next twenty-eight days, I worked like a madman! I was laser-focused like Rocky Balboa going into the championship round. I mapped out my exact plan on how I was going to get there. I needed to average close to $10,000 per day in commissions!

I didn't want to do it alone. Part of my income came from the sales volume of my entire sales team, and every dollar counted. I needed my entire sales team to step up like never before. So I organized a sales training the last two days of January and trained my team on successful sales strategies, including the B.A.N.K. system. I then launched an A-style contest to add some Nitro fuel to the fire.

I told the members of my sales team that if they hit certain benchmarks, they could win a Rolex watch! Now in my entire sales career, no one had ever given me a Rolex watch. I knew a Rolex was the symbol of success to an Action. I created a contest specifically designed for Actions. Everybody could play. I didn't single out the Blueprint or the Nurturing or the Knowledge types; they all got to compete too. But I specifically dangled the carrot to the Actions because I knew that would motivate them and shift them into massive action.

They had twenty-eight days to win it. Not only did I punch the pedal to the metal, but so did my sales team. It was amazing to see my team members step up and perform their very best, just to chase victory, win that competition, and reward themselves with their beautiful, new Rolex watches. I had five people win the contest that month—but the best part about it was that I not only achieved the unimaginable—but I exceeded it by $11,000, ending the month with a record-breaking $261,000 in income in twenty-eight days!

To this day, my record has never been beaten.

ACTION SUMMARY

Let's summarize the Action type. Actions are in a league of their own, and if you can learn to leverage that to your advantage, you're going to make a lot more bank. Action personality types typically have money to burn—or they at least want to create the illusion that they do. That can work in your favor, if you can catch them!

Action types never want to be limited by their finances, and they generally spend beyond their means. They're going to spend as much as they can possibly stretch and get away with. Don't bother going on and on about the cost or the budget. Actions don't care. They'll find a way to make things happen, if they want it badly enough. Your focus on the finances will only turn them off.

Start opening your mind to seeing what drives the Actions. They're high performance individuals. Think of a Ferrari. Think of a Lamborghini. Think of a Tesla. Think of super-high octane, and when you get into their world—you can sell into their world. Give them that red carpet treatment. Make them feel like they're absolute celebrities. If you don't have what it takes to close the deal with the Action, then find someone who does; ask for some help and have that person assist you in closing the process.

When you start landing and closing business with Actions, they're going to refer you into their inner circle, but only if you're cool like them. This is where you've got to step it up. I've told certain salespeople to go out and buy something expensive. Buy something that makes you look like you're successful. Go out and buy a designer dress or designer purse or designer shoes.

The same thing applied to me. I remember the first time I walked into Louis Vuitton. I'd always seen Louis Vuitton, and I wanted the high status of that brand. I'm an Action, but even I'd sit there and go, "Oh, my gosh! People actually spend that amount of money—more than $1,000—on shoes?" Oh, yes, they do! I was excited when I could finally afford my very first pair of designer shoes from Louis Vuitton. I was moving up in the world!

Actions live in the lap of luxury. Airlines sell first class seats for a reason—because Actions want the best of the best. Find something in your product mix that creates the best of the best. Take Actions to the nicest restaurants, the coolest places, and sell them a home while at the country club, not the real estate office. If you sell them the dream, you'll be able to live yours too.

Actions will outwork anyone, so they can out-earn everyone 2 to 1, 3 to 1, or even (according to the Word of Mouth Marketing Association) 57 to 1, simply so they can live the lifestyle others only fantasize about. If you can step into their world and sell into their world, you can do a lot more business.

EXERCISE

Memorize the twelve Action values and become fluent in the Action language.

Identify five things you can do to communicate and negotiate more effectively with an Action so you can close more sales:

1. ______________________________

2. ______________________________

3. ______________________________

4. ______________________________

5. ______________________________

NOTES

CHAPTER 12

NURTURING

RECYCLE THE BOX

"I don't think outside the box. I think of what I can do with the box."

— Author Unknown

Our third personality type is Nurturing. I like to classify Nurturing types as the ones who would *recycle the box*. They could also gift wrap the box and give it away, or even use the box to collect donations for the food bank or Toys for Tots. The key to Nurturing types is they care more about making a difference than they do about a dollar.

The color associated with Nurturing is yellow. They are warm people by nature, so I like to think of sunshine and sunflowers. They, like happy faces, are always smiling, and most importantly, they've got hearts of gold. Find a way to help them find purpose for their box.

UNDERSTANDING NURTURING TYPES

In order to use the right selling behaviors with Nurturing types, you need to understand their key motives, values, motivations, likes, dislikes, and typical behaviors. This section digs deeply into who Nurturing types are so you can better speak their language.

KEY MOTIVE

The key motive for the Nurturing type is to love and be loved! They truly do want to make the world a better place, and they believe that world peace is possible.

@CheriTree #WhyTheyBuy

Michael Jackson and Lionel Richie's song "We Are the World" reflects the utopian world the Nurturing type believes in. By giving, they believe they can make the world a better place. Find a way to connect and build meaningful relationships with the Nurturing and you'll have a customer and friend for life!

VALUES

There are twelve core values for Nurturing types:

1. Relationships
2. Authenticity
3. Personal growth
4. Significance
5. Teamwork
6. Involvement
7. Community
8. Charity
9. Ethics
10. Harmony
11. Morality
12. Contribution

Each value drives Nurturing types' decisions, and thus, their buying behavior. Let's review each of them in more detail so you understand the meaning and significance behind each Nurturing value.

RELATIONSHIPS

Relationships are the core of Nurturing types' business and the core of their lives. If a Nurturing type doesn't feel like she is connected to you and has a relationship with you, chances are slim to none that she'll actually buy from you. If you've ever heard of the saying, "People buy from people they like and trust," the nurturing personality type especially embodies that statement. The more you can create a relationship that's friendly and warm, the more you'll be able to move forward in the sales process.

AUTHENTICITY

Authenticity means that you're being genuine and real; not someone who is fake or misrepresenting him- or herself. Being authentic is really important to a Nurturing type, so you can't fake it 'til you make it when you're dealing with one. Sometimes in sales, there's an illusion that you have to come across as already ultra-successful and be able to flash the cash in order to do business. This is not true with Nurturing types. The more authentic you are, the faster you're going to connect with the hearts of your Nurturing prospect. Authenticity means that you also must be willing to be vulnerable. Authenticity is not something you can fake, so don't try. The more real and human you are, the more Nurturing types can relate to you, and therefore, the more likely they will be to do business with you.

PERSONAL GROWTH

Nurturing types live in an ideal world where the glass is always half-full. They're optimistic, and they like products and programs that create the feeling of personal growth so they can spread their wings and fly. They typically have a strong faith and are inspired to live their life purposes to the fullest, which often includes helping others, not just themselves. Personal growth is the sunshine for their souls.

SIGNIFICANCE

Nurturing types want their lives to have value and purpose, so they can make a difference, not just a dollar. Often, they want to make people feel significant, so they will go out of their way to serve others. They are a very selfless type of personality. They'll always give before they receive. They want to make sure you're okay, or that their spouse, children, community, church, or cause is getting the recognition and support it deserves.

They don't want the spotlight for the reasons of being egotistical or better than anyone else, but they do want to feel significant and appreciated in your eyes. If you give them simple acknowledgments, such as telling them thank you for their contributions, and letting them know you really appreciate them, then it's like giving sunshine to a flower. They'll literally perk up, open up, and become all that they can be with a little acknowledgment. Make sure you make them feel significant and you'll get much further ahead.

TEAMWORK

You've likely heard the saying, "Teamwork makes the dream work." TEAM is an acronym for Together Everyone Achieves More. Nurturing types really do believe this. If you isolate them at home or in their work environment where they're alone in a cubicle and completely disconnected from their peer group, they will underperform.

Nurturing types can struggle in home-based businesses if there's no one else for them to interact with. They want to be around the community, groups of people, and teams. If there is competition in the workplace or in the salesforce, the Nurturing type wants the whole team to win. They don't want to single out somebody as the champion so one person wins and everybody else loses. Their perfect scenario is a win-win situation.

INVOLVEMENT

Nurturing types have a disposition for service. They want to roll up their sleeves and contribute their time, money, and resources. They want to be involved in something greater than themselves. They want to feel involved, which means it's your goal to make them feel included. If you work with Nurturing types in your salesforce or company, get them involved as quickly as possible. The more they participate and add to the teamwork and culture, the more alive they become. If you ignore them or don't include them, they may shrivel up and die like a flower without sunshine.

COMMUNITY

Nurturing types love community. They love to belong to something, especially if it's something significant that has meaning, purpose, and makes a contribution to the world. Invite your Nurturing clients into your community or tribe. Your community might be your family or it could be the office group that goes out to lunch together. Make them feel included. Go out to the movies with them every now and then on the weekends. The more you create the feeling of community, the more progress you're going to make as you step deeper and deeper into their hearts, and, of course, that always leads to doing great business and receiving a lot of great referrals. If you don't have a tribe—build one!

CHARITY

The world is filled with the underprivileged, and it's the mission of the Nurturing types to make a difference. Typically, you'll find them volunteering or even working for non-profits. Even if their business is for-profit, they likely have a challenge being profitable because they prefer to give everything away. Because money plays a less significant role for them, Nurturing types keep score based on how much you or they donate to a good cause. If your company supports a charity, then remind them that a percentage of your profits goes to that charity.

If your company doesn't have a specific charity it supports, then find a way to support your favorite charity with your own time or money. You could offer your time toward a community service project once a quarter as a sales organization and invite your Nurturing clients to join you. Nurturing types want to see that you care about others and that you're committed to making a difference, not just a dollar.

ETHICS

Nurturing people care about other people, which means if you want to do business with Nurturing types, ethics should be at the core of your business, not just for you but for your entire company. Your products, services, or business opportunities need to have very high ethics and standards associated with them. If there's any type of "wolf in sheep's clothing" or someone who has the disposition to hurt others, be manipulative or dishonest, the Nurturing type will not get involved and will likely blow the whistle to protect others from being victimized.

HARMONY

Nurturing types value harmony for their families, communities, and even humanity. They call it world peace. This means they want to avoid any form of conflict, including possible conflict during the sales process. Their relationship with you is more important than money, products, services, or business opportunities. They would rather walk away from making money to avoid a conflict. This is typically why they also tend to give everything away. It's important to keep the peace with Nurturing types and not get caught up in debates or disagreements with them.

MORALITY

Nurturing types value clean, wholesome people, companies, and environments. Integrity is key for them because they don't want to see anyone get hurt. I've seen people resign and walk away from companies and careers simply because morals and scruples were lacking. Be sure to understand Nurturing types' moral boundaries and avoid anything that could be seen as immoral. If you honor and respect what is important to them, you'll go a lot further in the sales process and in building long-term relationships.

CONTRIBUTION

It all boils down to this: What are you or your company doing to make a difference, not just a dollar? You can see a theme here. Is greed driving your business, or your heart? While profit is important, it cannot be at the expense of other people. I've seen greed destroy companies, marriages, friendships, relationships, and more. Contribution is about making the world a better place, one person, one family, one community at a time.

In his book *Start With Why*, Simon Sinek emphasizes the importance of sharing why you are doing what you're doing. Sharing your purpose, vision, passion, and contribution to the world will connect your clients to you and enroll them into wanting to help support your mission. This is powerful and one of the top driving factors Nurturing types consider in selecting whom they align with in business.

OCCUPATIONS

Nurturing types look for careers or businesses based on their core values. Some of these occupations may include working with non-profits, nursing, social work, life coaching, volunteering, philanthropy, etc. Nurturing types want their work to make the world a better place. They support companies and organizations that are committed to making a difference and that put people before profits.

GREETING

When it comes to greeting the Nurturing type, you want to do it just right. The Blueprint greeting is too impersonal and the Action greeting is too aggressive and over the top. The best way to greet a Nurturing type is to give him or her a big, warm hug, heart to heart. If that's not appropriate, shake the person's hand with both hands and give friendly eye contact. They need to feel a genuine connection with you.

CLUES

One way to recognize a Nurturing type is to look for a particular set of clues, listed here.

- Loving Tones
- Always Touching
- Gives Hugs
- Positive and Happy
- Wears Soft Colors
- Dressed Comfortably
- Cheerful
- Unorganized (unless to impress)
- Wears Flowers or Costume Jewelry
- Friendly
- Talkative
- Helpful
- Thoughtful
- Drives Family Cars
- Maintains Eye Contact

LIKES

After surveying thousands of Nurturing types, I've created a list of their top likes and dislikes. This list of likes can help you identify the things they want or need as part of their buying language.

- A Good Cause
- Approval
- Authenticity
- Charity
- Children
- Counseling
- Diplomacy
- Empathy
- Encouragement
- Eye Contact

- Faith
- Familiarity
- Family
- Fresh Flowers
- Friends
- Helping
- Inspiration
- Intimacy
- Love
- Nature
- Peace
- Referrals
- Support
- Touching

DISLIKES

Just as the list above reveals the top items Nurturing types like, this list reveals their dislikes that you should avoid in your sales and communication process.

- Arguments
- Being Left Out
- Bullies
- Cold Shoulder
- Dead Flowers
- Deceit
- Dictators
- Disagreements
- Doing the Wrong Thing
- Egos
- Failure
- Fraud
- Greed
- Immorality
- Insincerity
- Lies
- Loneliness
- Manipulation
- Materialism
- Politics
- Rude Behavior
- Selling Tactics
- Tension
- Unfair Treatment

SUMMING UP THE NURTURING PERSONALITY

As you can see, Nurturing types are some of the friendliest and most open people around. They value relationships, which is why they won't trust you if there isn't a genuine connection. Nurturing types empower people to be their best and support others' growth. They believe there is more to life than money, which means that Nurturing types won't purchase unless there is a deeper purpose. When you remember Nurturing types' core personality and motivation, you'll understand *why they buy*.

NURTURING ASBS

Of course, just knowing what Nurturing types are like doesn't necessarily give you a roadmap for how to close a sale with Nurturing types. Luckily, specific adaptive selling behaviors have been proven to increase the likelihood of a successful sale with them. Following are some buying triggers and sales tips you can use to get the yes from people who identify as Nurturing.

BUYING TRIGGERS

Our independent research studies analyzed the top buying triggers (actions, facts, or realities established during the buying process that trigger a yes) for each code. Here are the Top Five Buying Triggers for those whose dominant code is Nurturing:

1. Knowing the company makes a contribution to a worthwhile cause.

2. Knowing they're buying the best possible goods or services.
3. Positive recommendations from people they know.
4. A high-quality presentation of the product or service.
5. Excellent written details describing the product or service.

SALES TIPS

Using the right buying triggers alone isn't enough, though. Now that you understand more about Nurturing types, you've got to use the right ASBs in every step of the sales process to close the sale. These are key sales tips and strategies that I want to recommend to you. Each of these selling behaviors will help you build better rapport, speak Nurturing types' language, and increase the chance of closing your sale.

- Be authentic and genuine.
- Show them you care more about them than money.
- Introduce them to your team and get them connected with others in the group.
- Talk about the cause you are passionate about and how they can make a difference.
- Give big hugs or a warm greeting.
- Maintain good eye contact.

EMBRACING YOUR INNER NURTURING

Now that you understand who Nurturing types are and how to sell to them successfully, it's time to leverage your own inner Nurturing side to drive more sales. I'm going to share some amazing success stories from my own life and from other inspiring B.A.N.K. clients to show you how leveraging the Nurturing code can massively increase your sales success. Then, I'll summarize everything you've learned about Nurturing types with some final strategies for closing sales with them.

SUCCESS STORY - NANI G.

I want to share a success story about a woman named Wainani Kailialoha Marrotte-Gomes (Nani Gomes for short). Nani is from the beautiful state of Hawaii. Hawaii is celebrated for its "Aloha," which translates to love, respect, and caring—all part of Hawaii's nurturing culture. It's one of my favorite places to have lived!

When I met Nani, she was working as an independent distributor in the direct sales and network marketing industry. She had signed up with a number of different companies over the years, trying to build a business with significant income potential, always believing that each company was The One. It was easy for Nani to fall in love with the people in the company, the products they offered, and the purpose they shared. However, as great as that was, she rarely enjoyed the financial profits.

For years, Nani made very little income. In the beginning, that wasn't an issue; she believed building relationships was the key to greater financial success, and it wasn't truly the money that motivated her. However, it became an issue when times got tough, Nani's family began to hurt financially, her home was headed to foreclosure, and her family relationships suffered. She was in need of a miracle.

Nani heard about my company and called to learn more about B.A.N.K. She wanted to see whether it was a tool that could help her attract the right people to her business and make more money. She did have one condition before agreeing to use the B.A.N.K. system to grow her business—she wanted to make sure it was not based upon any form of manipulation or unethical sales tactics. I appreciated her concern, and I explained how B.A.N.K. was simply based on understanding the customer's values and having the respect to deliver a presentation based on what was more important to him or her. This made complete sense to her so she began using it immediately.

In a short time, Nani experienced unprecedented success for herself and her family. Using the B.A.N.K. training, she was able to surround herself with the right kind of people and build her team, increasing sales the following year and earning well over $100,000 for the first time in her life! This was life-changing income for Nani...but the success didn't end there.

B.A.N.K. not only improved Nani's business and income, but it also improved her relationships with her husband and family. B.A.N.K. taught Nani how to speak the language of people, which encouraged beneficial communication between her and her family members. In fact, it made such an impact on her life that she decided to become one of our certified trainers so she could share it with the rest of her world.

Nani has shared B.A.N.K. with her sales teams, her family, and her friends with the intention of teaching as many people the language of people as possible. Although B.A.N.K. was originally designed to increase sales, it has the proven ability to impact lives on a personal level. Committed to making a difference, Nani shared B.A.N.K. with two Honolulu Police Department officers, Taylor Ho'opii and Don Faumuina, who were working on getting kids off the streets and into beneficial youth programs. These two men embraced the B.A.N.K. system and got certified to teach it to adults, community leaders, and even members of the Hawaiian government with the purpose of creating a community that could communicate effectively.

B.A.N.K. is changing lives around the world every single day. Nani lives the essence of B.A.N.K. and is doing her part to support our mission of ONE WORLD—ONE LANGUAGE.

Not long ago, I was deeply moved by a story Nani shared with me about a family who was temporarily displaced and living in an office. Nani felt the need to reach out and open up her home to them until they could relocate back to the mainland. This loving family often faced challenges due to poor communication and working through strong differences in opinions. Their only son struggled the most and often felt alone, isolated, disconnected, and at one point, he contemplated suicide. Although Nani's not a psychologist or family therapist, she was able to teach the family members about each of their B.A.N.K. codes and how they impacted the family's personal dynamics. After taking the assessment and learning about the differences between the codes, they discovered that the father was a strong A, mom was a high B, the grandmother a high N, and the son was a K who was often stuck in his head and conflicted. Once I explained the codes and how they impact each other, everything changed. The son shifted his perspective of himself, and with a new self-esteem, he proclaimed to his family that he now understands he's not "broken," he's just a "K"—and by the way, he's smarter than all of them! This family's life was changed because of B.A.N.K.

HOW I USED MY NURTURING SIDE FOR SUCCESS

Nurturing values can help anyone, not just high-level N's like Nani. When I was starting out in sales, I was all about the close. I wanted to get to the point fast and make the sale. Chatting with others is great, but that wasn't why I was there, and I wanted to get to the point. This straight-to-the-point approach worked great with A's and B's, and K's were just happy I wasn't boring them with small talk, but N's seemed to be turned off by this approach. They needed to feel a connection before they were willing to buy.

That's why I had to embrace my N. Luckily, I am high N too, which made it much easier to integrate it into the way I do business. I just had to be more intentional about it.

When I was in sales, I always made team-building activities a priority—for my own sales team, for my clients, and for my entire network. Our team-building activities became a weekly tradition. We would go to late-night movies after training days, spend time on the weekends as a group going to yacht fests or on dream home tours, and I even scheduled one-on-one lunch dates with each salesperson on my team to make sure everyone had the support he or she needed.

Sure, some of these meetings had secondary goals, too. I used the weekend events to sell the dream, and my one-on-ones also allowed me to keep tabs on my team's progress. For the N's, though, any other goals of the community-building activities didn't matter. I was genuinely reaching out to connect with the team, and they appreciated the gesture. Even simple recognition of a job well-done went far with my N team members. A thank you from the heart showed them I appreciated their work—and who they were as individuals.

Community-building activities were vital to reaching N clients, as well. I already told you about the parties I used to throw at my luxury house to appeal to A's, but what I didn't tell you is that this was also a way I tapped into my inner N. You see, these big parties were a chance for me to connect with my greater network, and I used them as such. I always thanked everyone genuinely for visiting my home, and I made it clear I was there to serve, but I never sold anything at my parties. This let me get to know potential clients as people, not simply prospects.

When people left my parties, they were always impressed by how much fun they had and how great it was to relax in the presence of so many people who had shared goals and dreams. It was an authentic way to include new guests into the community without pressuring them to buy before they were ready. It was a great way for them to get to know me personally, off the stage and away from a microphone.

For people who weren't interested in parties, I did alternative client appreciation events. My favorite option was to do community service together. We would go to a food bank and feed the homeless on a Saturday or complete some other project. I was able to make a difference while showing my clients what causes I valued. Serving others together showed my philanthropic side, and it was an opportunity to bond over those shared values.

When I was in my early twenties, I volunteered as a missionary in Romania and did a lot of service projects—from feeding the hungry to visiting the orphanages and holding babies who didn't have anyone to love them. This always made me feel really good and it gave me a sense of purpose that was far more meaningful than just achieving financial success. As the years went by, I always made it a point to focus on doing my small part to make the world a better place, and doing it as a team was even more rewarding.

I quickly learned that constantly building my community was a great way to drive sales. For one thing, my network expanded exponentially, especially when I reached out to N's. N's may not care about money, but they have plenty of social capital—and an N's network is open to you if you genuinely earn his or her trust by building up teams through real outreach and offering true camaraderie and friendship.

I now make sure I am always doing something to build up the community. I love to get the tribe together and serve every member of my team, every client, and every person in my network like he or she is part of my family. This is full N, and it has helped me build lasting success. After all, sales is all about people—and N's know a lot of people!

NURTURING SUMMARY

Let's summarize the Nurturing type. They are warm, friendly, loving, good, salt-of-the-earth people. Treat them like your friends, or, even better, really good friends. Sell to them based on what's truly in their best interests, and come from a place of authenticity. Be vulnerable by sharing with them from your heart why you're doing what you're doing, and how it's your personal mission to share your products with the world.

Be willing to tap into the Nurturing part of your code and connect it to the Nurturing part of your client's code. This will allow you to create an important connection in that relationship, creating a compelling reason to do business with you.

Nurturing types make buying decisions with their hearts, guts, and intuition. Have you ever heard someone say, "I can't quite put my finger on it, but I just don't feel right about doing this"? Or you may have heard the opposite, "I can't quite put my finger on it, but it just feels right to do this."

You hear this all the time in sales. That's a surefire clue that you're talking to a Nurturing type. Nurturing types make their decisions with their hearts, not with their heads, their egos, or their wallets. Find your heart. Grow it three times as big before you have an appointment with the Nurturing type. When you do, you'll create an experience that feels like it wasn't a sales process at all. It will simply feel like you're helping a friend.

If you struggle with tapping into your Nurturing code, there are many personal development seminar programs you can attend, audios to listen to, or books to read. You can even attend yoga classes and learn about your chakras. Although this may sound a little "woo-woo" for you, such activities are important if you want to build strong relationships with Nurturing types.

Somewhere inside of you there's an amazing reason for being. There's a much higher purpose than just simply making money and taking it to the bank. You're looking for the way you're able to change a life. The company or the product you represent is worthy of that conversation.

Another little secret is, if you really don't believe in what you're selling—if it's just simply a job that pays the bills—that might be the problem. Start now to find a different place to work and a better way to live. You can't live with yourself every day all day knowing that you're selling something that is hurting a potential customer and dissatisfying to you in any way. Find something that lifts you up, that makes you feel good about yourself.

Most importantly, understand that although your Nurturing client may not have access to many financial resources because money isn't important to him, that doesn't make him a bad client. The opposite is actually true. I've found that Nurturing types trade in an alternate currency—relationship currency. Whom they're connected to and whom they have access to can be worth its weight in gold—as long as you treat them right, according to their code.

EXERCISE

Memorize the twelve Nurturing values and become fluent in the Nurturing language.

Identify five things you can do to communicate and negotiate more effectively, and close more sales with a Nurturing type:

1. ____

2. ____

3. ____

4. ____

5. ____

NOTES

CHAPTER 13

KNOWLEDGE

ENGINEER THE BOX

"One of the only ways to get out of a tight box is to invent your way out."

– Jeff Bezos

Our final code is Knowledge. I like to classify the Knowledge types as the ones who would *engineer the box*. They are bright with beautiful minds and are fully capable of working with the most complex problems and bringing innovative solutions to the table.

The color associated with Knowledge is green. Knowledge types are extremely logical and love enormous amounts of data, so I think of Microsoft Excel's green logo. Knowledge types love computers and coding, which I associate with the green code on the screen in the movie *The Matrix*. Knowledge types are so innovative they build cars that run on electricity instead of gasoline, which uses green technology.

UNDERSTANDING KNOWLEDGE TYPES

In order to use the right selling behaviors with Knowledge types, you need to understand their key motives, values, motivations, likes, dislikes, and typical behaviors. This section digs deep into who Knowledge types are so you can better speak their language.

KEY MOTIVE

The key motive for the Knowledge type is to be right! They cannot ever be wrong, and therefore, they will not move forward with your offer unless they know with certainty that it is the right decision.

@CheriTree #WhyTheyBuy

This can be challenging, and it often leads to lengthy discussions and even heated debates. Look for ways to help your Knowledge prospect discover the right way to move forward, and you'll close the sale a lot faster than usual.

VALUES

There are twelve core values for Knowledge:

1. Learning
2. Intelligence
3. Logic
4. Self-Mastery
5. Technology
6. Research and Development
7. Science
8. Universal Truths
9. Expertise
10. Competence
11. Accuracy
12. The Big Picture

Each value drives Knowledge types' decisions, and thus, their buying behavior. Let's review each value in more detail so you understand the meaning and significance behind it.

LEARNING

Knowledge types love to learn. If they could, they'd eat information for breakfast, lunch, and dinner. Imagine if they could install little USB ports inside the backs of their heads and simply plug into the Internet every night to download unlimited bits of data—they would love it. They would hot-sync to that machine every single night just to know everything. They love to learn, which means if you're selling to them something that's information-based, they're likely going to be interested. In fact, one of my Knowledge friends used to put books underneath his pillow at night as a kid, hoping to learn through osmosis!

INTELLIGENCE

Knowledge types are intelligent people. They're very, very smart. Typically, as a parent, you get notified very early if your child is above the learning curve and his or her IQ is higher than average. Sometimes these children get placed into special programs in school systems. They get extra attention based on their intellect. Knowledge teenagers usually start taking advanced and even college-level classes while still in high school. They're just intellectually superior and, therefore, they value other people's intelligence.

Intelligence shows up in the genius of your thought and your ability to articulate complex concepts. It shows up in the way you can process different points of view or analyze everything from every angle. Whereas Blueprints are very matter of fact—black and white—Knowledge types live in the gray matter. They can see things from every angle and formulate their ideas to create a solution. This is what makes them geniuses, and they expect the same in return.

LOGIC

The definition of the word logic is reasoning conducted or assessed according to strict principles of validity. In other words, for Knowledge types, logic means that everything you say or do must make sense. If your sales presentation does not make sense, they're not going to buy. If your business opportunity doesn't make sense, they won't join, or if your financial model isn't logical, they won't move forward.

Logic can impact the entire outcome of your sales presentation. Let me explain. Let's say you're delivering your presentation and going through points A, B, C, D, E, etc. At point C, you say something that is confusing to the Knowledge type and breaks with logic. What you shared didn't make sense. This is where you lose the sale. Picture a train going down the track, and at point C, it goes off track and is no longer able to follow you down the track to points D, E, F, G, H, I, and so on.

This creates something called *split thinking*. You might get all the way to Z, finish your presentation, and be ready to ask for the sale, but your Knowledge prospect is still stuck all the way back at point C where you broke with logic. In this case, you've confused him or her out of a sale. After all, a confused mind buys nothing. Make sure you stay logical the entire way and allow the K's to ask questions.

SELF-MASTERY

Knowledge types can have extreme focus and discipline on topics that interest them, and they can take it to a level of self-mastery. For example, if they're studying martial arts, they're not going to stop with their white belt or yellow belt—but they'll take it all the way to black belt or multiple degrees of black belt. Whether it's martial arts, music, physics, or academics, self-mastery is a must. If you use that analogy when you're representing your products and services, you'll understand that Knowledge types want to do business with an expert who has taken their studies or business to a level of mastery.

TECHNOLOGY

Without a doubt, technology has shaped nearly every aspect of the way we live and work today. From the way we communicate with one another and the way we travel from one location to another to the way we obtain and share information, we are constantly relying on technology to simplify our most basic daily activities, and this is why the Knowledge types love it! Cutting-edge technology can shape the world we live in and take us into new dimensions. Look at what Steve Jobs did for our mobile communication world by coming out with the iPhone. He literally revolutionized our world through smart technology. Technology is fascinating to Knowledge types and intrigues them to want to learn more. Find ways to connect your customer to your technology.

RESEARCH AND DEVELOPMENT

Often called R&D, Research and Development is a general term for activities in connection with corporate or governmental innovation. It is situated at the front end of the innovation life cycle, which may end with commercialization.

Knowledge types love innovation and value companies that invest a lot into Research and Development, searching for theories and proving them, testing them, conducting clinical trials, studies, etc. Knowledge types value the research that comes from studying and analyzing data so they can discover more and more, and use this information to build everything from technology to spaceships or even attempt to find the cure to cancer.

SCIENCE

Science is a systematic enterprise that builds and organizes knowledge in the form of testable explanations and predictions about the universe. Knowledge types are attracted to science because they want to understand how and why everything works. A child who likes to take things apart and rebuild them likely has a very high K score. She might disassemble the toaster or want to dissect a frog. As an adult, she may study anatomy and become a doctor. Knowledge types want to use science to learn how things work and to try to find a better way to solve challenges. B.A.N.K is based in personality science that has its origins in Hippocratic teachings. Thousands of years of study have given personality science the foundation necessary to gain traction in the modern world.

UNIVERSAL TRUTHS

Universal Truth is considered to be universal if it is valid in all times and places. In this case, it is seen as eternal or absolute. The reason Knowledge types value universal truths is no one can argue with them. Instead, everyone accepts them as true. Therefore, it's imperative that your presentation is built on a foundation of universal truths. Do not start off your presentation with an idea that is not validated as a universal truth. Doing so could unravel your theory and subject you to a lot of unnecessary debating.

EXPERTISE

Knowledge types value expertise and expect you to be a subject-matter expert (SME) on your topic or in your field. They respect SMEs because of what it takes to become an SME. If you're not an expert, you could be considered a fool, and therefore, you will definitely lose the sale. K can also stand for know-it-all. It's likely that your Knowledge type client knows more than the average person on your product topic, and therefore, you need to ramp up your knowledge significantly to meet him at or above his level. If you are not perceived as the expert, you will likely not have the credibility needed to close the sale.

COMPETENCE

Knowledge types have very little patience with incompetence. They expect you to be competent at describing your products and services, and deliver a presentation that demonstrates your competence. I've seen a lot of salespeople lose the sale simply due to a lack of competence. For example, if you're doing a product demonstration but you don't know how the equipment works, you won't close the sale. If you can't get your technology to cooperate with you, you'll likely lose the sale.

When I was selling insurance and investments, I absolutely needed to make sure I knew how to fill out the paperwork. As part of the life insurance process, if I was selling an insurance policy under a certain financial threshold where we didn't need to gather a blood sample, I simply needed to get a saliva sample. To do so, I had to administer something called a spit kit, where I took out a swab, put it in the customer's mouth, and collected his or her saliva. Then I had to put it into a test tube, packaged it, and mailed it off to the lab where it would be tested to determine whether the client qualified for the insurance. This wasn't necessarily fun for me, but I did need to be competent throughout the entire process if I wanted to get paid.

ACCURACY

Think of Knowledge types' brains as computers. They are programmed to solve problems and find errors. They can't help it—which means they can't overlook it if they find errors in your work too. If your math is off by a number, or your spelling or grammar has a mistake, Knowledge types are compelled to point it out. Such errors can also be a deal breaker. I've overheard Knowledge types admit that if they find an error in the presentation, marketing material, or even the website—they won't buy the products—because, "If they're this careless here, then they're likely to be careless with the product too." Case in point, one of my Knowledge friends was an English professor. He would tell his students that if he was in charge of hiring and they had a typo in a resume, he would not hire them!

THE BIG PICTURE

Knowledge types need to see the big picture before they can bury themselves down in the nitty-gritty details. Explaining the big picture allows for the use of logic and reason required before launching into the project. K's prefer to be guided by a bigger goal, not focused on satisfying the minor, detailed steps toward the goal. To understand the importance of the big picture, let's look at how NASA put a man on the moon.

On May 25, 1961, President John F. Kennedy announced a plan to put an American safely on the moon before the end of the decade. At the time, few people thought this goal could be achieved. After all, we had none of the necessary technology. Still, an ambitious team of NASA engineers who saw the big picture believed it could be achieved with hard work and the right resources.

You see, Kennedy had been feeling great pressure to catch up to the Soviet Union in the Space Race. The Cold War wasn't going so well for the Americans, especially in light of the recent Bay of Pigs fiasco, so the president needed a big win. Scientists at NASA embraced the massive undertaking, eventually making the Apollo project a success when Apollo 11 commander Neil Armstrong took his first steps on the moon in 1969.

Once the team of engineers understood the big picture and the importance for the U.S. to be the first country in the world to put a man on the moon, they got to work and built the first spacecraft that could travel to the moon safely—and return! This very "K" perspective allowed the team to put everything toward a future goal guided by the bigger picture. It truly was, "One small step for man, one giant leap for mankind."

Watch the movie, or read the book, *Hidden Figures* to see how a team of K's actually cracked the space travel code. Fascinating!

OCCUPATIONS

Knowledge types look for careers or businesses based on their core values. Some of these occupations may include engineering, science, programming, research, and analyst positions. It's important to Knowledge types to work in environments where they can be creative and innovative, and use their brains. They appreciate working with other smart people and don't have patience for mindless work.

GREETING

Greeting the Knowledge type can be tricky. They are not fans of too much touch or intimacy. They'd much prefer you greet them with a simple head nod or handing over a business card rather than a handshake. They are very particular about their personal space, so don't make the mistake of getting too close. This is a classic case where *less is more.*

CLUES

One way to recognize a Knowledge type is to look for a particular set of clues, listed here.

- Quiet/Reserved
- Lost in Thought
- Gadgets
- Techy Talk
- Wallflowers
- Complicated Conversations
- Technical Reading
- Shares Expertise
- Wardrobe Malfunction
- Internet Junkie
- Drives Electric or High Performance Cars
- Watches Sci-fi
- Always Reading
- Intellectual Debates
- Plays Computer Games

LIKES

After surveying thousands of Knowledge types, I created a list of their top likes and dislikes. This likes list can help you identify the things they want or need as part of their buying language.

- Analysis
- Charts and Graphs
- Consumer Reports
- Data
- Documentation
- Experts
- Facts
- Formulas
- Gadgets
- Higher Education
- Information
- Innovation
- Logic
- Maps
- Peer Journals
- Proof
- Puzzles
- Research and Development
- Science Fiction
- Software
- Strategy
- Studies
- Technology
- Wit

DISLIKES

Just as the list above reveals the top items the Knowledge likes, this list reveals the dislikes you should avoid in your sales and communication process.

- Automated Recommendations
- Blanket Statements
- Celebration
- Celebrity Endorsements
- Chitchat
- Drama
- Emotions
- Excessive Praise
- Excitement

- Ignorance
- Incompetence
- Lack of Documentation
- Networking
- Poor Listeners
- Public Speaking
- Recognition
- Role Playing
- Shortcuts
- Social Media Buzz
- Social Mixers
- Speculation
- Stupidity
- Touching
- Unsubstantiated Evidence

SUMMING UP THE KNOWLEDGE PERSONALITY

As you can see, Knowledge types are some of the smartest and most rational people around. They value reason, which gives them an uncanny ability to analyze a situation quickly and accurately. Knowledge types have a lifelong quest for self-mastery, so they are constantly looking to improve. They'll happily analyze difficult topics and take all the raw data to which you can give them access. When you remember Knowledge types' core personality and motivation, you'll understand *why they buy.*

KNOWLEDGE ASBS

Of course, just knowing what Knowledge types are like doesn't necessarily give you a roadmap for how to close a sale with them. Luckily, specific adaptive selling behaviors have been proven to increase the likelihood of a successful sale with K types. The following are some buying triggers and sales tips you can use to get the yes from Knowledge types.

BUYING TRIGGERS

Our independent research studies analyzed the top buying triggers (actions, facts, or realities established during the buying process that trigger a yes) for each code. Here are the Top Five Buying Triggers for those whose primary code is Knowledge:

1. Staying within their budget.
2. Having time to do full due diligence on the purchase.
3. Having all the information they need to make the smartest decision possible.
4. Excellent written details describing the product or service.
5. Knowing they're buying the best possible goods or services.

SALES TIPS

Using the right buying triggers alone isn't enough, though. Now that you understand more about Knowledge types, you've got to use the right ASBs in every step of the sales process to close the sale. Following are key sales tips and strategies that will help you build better rapport with Knowledge types, speak their language, and increase the chance of closing your sale.

- Be smart and know your information.

- Have resources and documentation that you can provide for them to study.
- Stay logical in your approach, and don't get overly emotional or excited.
- Be able to debate and defend your product, service, or business, or bring someone with you who is more of an expert.
- Allow them to do their own research and give them time to think about it.
- Stay within budget.

EMBRACING YOUR INNER KNOWLEDGE

Now that you understand who Knowledge types are and how to sell to them successfully, it's time to leverage your own inner Knowledge to drive more sales. I'm going to share some amazing success stories from my own life and from other smart B.A.N.K. clients to show you how leveraging the Knowledge code can massively increase your sales success. Then, I'll summarize everything you've learned about Knowledge types with some final strategies for closing the sale with them.

KNOWLEDGE SUCCESS STORY

Let me share two success stories from our B.A.N.K. clients.

SUCCESS STORY – EDWARD T.

My wife, Raquel, and I were hosting some of our insurance company's best clients at a local Ruth's Chris Steak House. The purpose of the evening was to sell those in attendance on the value of long-term care insurance. Long-term insurance policies are complex policies that normally take multiple meetings to unpack the many intricacies included. This dinner meeting was the first attempt at dinner information sessions that Raquel and I had put together. We had a plan.

Once everyone was seated, Raquel and I would go to a table and code each of the couples individually. We had just completed our B.A.N.K. training a few weeks prior. After collecting the B.A.N.K. codes of all our clients, we noticed we had all four codes represented. Before the meeting began, we took the product specialist for the meeting aside and guided him on how he should lean the tenor of the presentation to speak to all codes. Our product specialist from our carrier gave his presentation. The presentation for the evening went off beautifully with a number of questions at the end. At the end of the evening, we gathered level-of-interest postcards from each couple. One couple stated a willingness to discuss the insurance further.

I set up a meeting with this couple to discuss their needs. The husband's code was KABN and the wife's code was NABK. Prior to the meeting, I discussed with my product specialist, who was assisting me on the case, the BANK codes and what they meant. Additionally, we went on to discuss a plan for how to approach and work with the couple. Understanding that the husband's first code was Knowledge, I immediately instructed my product specialist to send all illustrations and documentation to the client ahead of the meeting, allowing the husband the opportunity to review them.

We met the couple at their office. I sat across from the wife and my product specialist sat across from the husband. Our intent was to allow me to connect with the wife on the relationship she and I had developed over the years while the husband grilled my product specialist on the specific details of the long-term care/life insurance policy we were there to discuss. The meeting lasted for ninety minutes. The wife and I talked about her dogs. Her husband and my product specialist discussed the coverage in heavy detail.

At the end of the meeting, the husband leaned back in his seat, looked at his wife, smiled, and said, "We can do two $50,000 long-term care policies, and we will use the money from that property we are selling to pay for it." We scheduled one additional follow-up call to review the few changes the clients wanted to tailor coverages. Our next meeting was to sign the final documents and collect payment. We netted $20,000 in commission for this case. It took one dinner meeting, one face-to-face meeting, and a follow-up call!

After I took my product specialist back to pick up the check, he stopped me before we got in the car to leave and said, "That is the fastest I have ever gotten two long-term care polices closed with checks as well. That was awesome."

Would we have closed this case without B.A.N.K.? Maybe. But we would not have closed it as fast. B.A.N.K. provided us a system that we have repeated to close our sales faster.

SUCCESS STORY – BRETT Y.

B.A.N.K. helped me in two very powerful ways. One, it helped me close some deals faster and for more money. Two, it dramatically improved my personal relationships, but most importantly, it improved my relationship with my wife.

I sell large computer technology systems. I have one customer who has bought our products on a semi-regular basis, but it is not uncommon for it to take 12-24 months to close a deal with this customer. In early fall of last year, we found out that this customer might want to upgrade a system, so we worked out proposals and did a number of presentations to them. I was really hoping that they might be willing to buy before the end of the year, but it did not seem to be in the cards. The net result of these presentations was that while the customer seemed interested in our proposal for about $1.5 million, we were told "No, not now, but perhaps next year." They were not motivated to buy at that time.

A couple of weeks later, I took one of the B.A.N.K. live training programs, and started to think about all the people I dealt with, what their personality types were, and what motivated them. During the training, I noted that most of the people we dealt with at this customer's company were very much Blueprint types, with lots of planning, procedures, structures, and systems, and all in the service of avoiding risk. My top two personality codes are Knowledge and Action, and I realized that some of my biggest lost deals and challenges in my career were with Blueprint-style customers.

One week after I returned from the training, this same customer called us with an idea unrelated to the previous discussion. They wanted to extend the life of a different very old system by using decommissioned systems from another location. They only needed to extend the capacity on that system for a twelve-month period. They asked for our help in planning this. During this discussion, a light bulb went off in my head. What they were thinking was risky…and the Blueprint personality wants to avoid risk. While they could move decommissioned components around, since they owned them, they were not under support by our company any more. They could be brought back into support, but that would be expensive to do, and also time-consuming. We asked lots of questions about this plan of theirs, which uncovered all the hidden risks, costs, and time delays (which meant more risk and costs). The customer started to get very uncomfortable with all the risks and asked us for alternative suggestions.

My team came up with a counter-proposal. We suggested that they buy the *new* systems they already planned to buy, but to buy them this year instead of waiting for next year… and use some of the systems to extend the current system for their immediate needs. Then they could redeploy those systems for the new system only after a year…. Since these were all *new* systems and *fully supported*, we had reduced the risk for them. They could also get this done much faster. Also, they were already planning on buying next year, so it was not an extra cost; it was simply spending the money sooner. But one other thing happened. During the planning process, they starting extrapolating all their long-terms needs, and they determined they needed even more equipment, which increased the size of the order by another $1 million, to about $2.5 million. They placed the order in December of last year—one year ahead of schedule, and for $1 million more than originally planned. It was exactly what they wanted because it reduced their risk. We were able to close the deal much faster and for more money, simply by presenting our ideas in a manner that emphasized what was important to them. We went through all the details and did careful planning together with them, and we highlighted what the risks and potential risks were of their initial idea, and then we helped them discover a new plan and new proposal that would reduce their risks and meet their timelines.

Bottom line: By understanding that this customer had many Blueprint-style decision makers, we were able to show them an alternate plan that reduced their risks and gave them a much safer plan, and in the process, they decided to *buy now* instead of waiting another year. By focusing on reducing their risk, we motivated them to buy now. They also decided to place an order that was 66 percent larger when we explored the plan in detail with them.

The second area where B.A.N.K. has had a huge impact in my life is my relationship with my wife. My wife came with me to a short B.A.N.K. introductory training, and then I went on to learn B.A.N.K. in depth over the next six months, taking additional live training. My wife and I both came to a deeper understanding and respect for what is different and unique about each of us. Knowledge and Action are the highest codes for me, but Blueprint and Nurturer are the highest codes for my wife. My wife and I balance each other out in most situations, but there were situations about money and investments where we conflicted, and that could cause some conflicts and fights. After learning B.A.N.K., we now have deeper understanding, empathy, and respect for each other. This had led to higher quality money decisions, and it has also created much more harmony and love in our relationship. It really has deepened our harmony and teamwork in many areas of our relationship, and not just money and investments. B.A.N.K. has helped deepen our self-awareness of our own personality codes, and it has increased our mutual awareness, understanding, empathy, and love for each other. We are as deeply in love now as ever, even after twenty-one years of marriage.

B.A.N.K. has helped me make more money with customers who used to be a challenge for me to relate to, and B.A.N.K. has also helped me have more love in my life. What more could I ask for? I can take that to the BANK, and I can also take that to my HEART!

HOW I USED MY KNOWLEDGE SIDE FOR SUCCESS

They say, "Knowledge is power." Consequently, anyone can use K-level expertise to succeed, just like Brett did. When I decided to become a financial advisor, I was far from an expert. Unfortunately, selling financial services isn't exactly a field where you can just wing it. You must pass several exams to get the right certifications before you can even get started, and once you begin your career, you must become extremely knowledgeable about every product you sell. After all, there's no way anyone is going to turn over his or her entire portfolio to you if you don't know what you're talking about.

I am not a super-high K, but I knew I'd have to tap deeply into my K side to build a successful career selling financial services. I'd have to be super-competent and knowledge-able about all our products if I wanted people to trust me with their savings, their financial health, and their future. It was tough at first, but I was motivated to make it. I put my A-style "I can do anything" attitude toward becoming the best K that I could be in this area.

I started studying like crazy. I was determined to become a subject-matter expert. I read everything I could get my hands on that had anything to do with insurance, financial services, real estate, investing, and personal finance. Books, articles, prospectuses, newspaper articles, everything. You name it, I probably read it. I even forced myself to read ev-ery line of the fine print in contracts for financial products and packages to find every "gotcha" clause that would cost my customers money.

Beyond the reading, my days were filled with learning op-portunities. I met with fund managers and industry experts on a regular basis to find out what the newest trends were. I attended lectures and conferences on economics, Wall Street, finance, real estate, and everything in between. I invested countless hours of my "free time" in attending presentations, running comparative analyses, and sifting through endless stacks of customer financial data.

I became a dedicated attendee of my company's "Saturday school" to develop a deeper understanding of what it meant to be the best financial advisor. Every Saturday, my company offered a half-day training on a topic related to the insurance industry, financial services, or sales. For five solid years, I attended those classes, soaking in all the knowledge available about my chosen field and propelling myself to mastery.

If you're a K, that might sound like fun, but for me, it certainly was not. To tell you the truth, it makes me want to cringe when I think about it. There were many times when I would have preferred to skip the training and go golfing, skiing, or do just about anything else than studying! But it was all worth it in the end. I needed to embrace my inner K to become a knowledgeable financial advisor whom all my customers could trust.

It worked. Over the course of those five years, I went from a naive salesperson, who was trying to fake it 'til I made it, to a true expert. I knew the products we offered inside and out. You could have asked me just about any question related to our field and I could quickly provide an informed, accurate answer. When I compared different products to each other or our products with those of our competitors, I felt sure of my analysis. This gave me much more confidence—and it made closing the sale much easier with any customer.

To most customers, I had the expertise needed to show them that I could serve them well as a financial advisor without having to give them raw data for proof. Still, even this level of knowledge and competence in the field wasn't enough for K customers. They needed to be part of the analysis. While my competence reassured them that I was worth listening to, simply trusting my expertise wasn't good enough. I had to double down on the data and knowledge to provide more to them.

To sell to K customers, I collected every single data point that could be relevant to the specific financial services I was selling. I sent them relevant research, recent newspaper articles, information from industry experts, mutual fund prospectuses, stock market analyses, and any of that kind of data in print or digital form. I learned that when K's ask to see more data, you don't give them just a little bit more information. You inundate them with data.

You see, for a K, more data is always better. They can choose to look it all over or not, but they will appreciate getting the full picture. Now that my days as a financial advisor are long over, I still keep this policy in place. When I find out that someone is a K, I don't hold back on the data I give him or her about B.A.N.K. I send K's our white paper, our published studies—everything. There is no such thing as too much information to a K, and my knowledge becomes my power—the power to get the yes!

KNOWLEDGE SUMMARY

Let's summarize the Knowledge type. Of all the four personality types, Knowledge types can be the most difficult to sell to for most people, and they typically have the longest sales cycle. There's a reason for this. They do not make emotional decisions—they make logical decisions. The higher the emotions—the less likely they are to buy. Knowledge types have a saying to live by, "When emotions are high, logic is low." Therefore, it's very important that you prepare for your presentations and deliver them based in logic and common sense. When you demonstrate a very logical reason for buying your products, you will close the sale much faster.

I want to share some insight about why it can be more difficult to sell to the Knowledge types. If you've ever felt like your Knowledge prospect is taking too long to make a buying decision, asks too many questions, or gets stuck in analysis paralysis—it's because of this one factor—he or she cannot be wrong!

From a very early age, Knowledge types were identified in school systems as being special—gifted—because of their high IQs. They started getting special attention and took advanced courses based on their above-average intelligence. They developed a thirst for learning, studying, and even testing. They acquired high self-esteem based on how much they knew, and they worked hard to make sure they were never wrong.

As they matured into adult life, they based their decision-making on facts and data to ensure they would never be wrong. They trust information more than emotions. This explains why they need so much information to make a buying decision—because their egos will not allow them to be wrong. You need to show them that choosing you definitely won't be a mistake.

K's can be some of the toughest nuts to crack because you can't close them. They have to close themselves. You can help them get there faster by presenting your information competently and giving them all the data they need to see why your offer is the best solution.

Ultimately, you won't be able to close any sale if your product is simply the wrong fit for your prospect, but with K's, the logic has to be even more foolproof. You won't convince them to buy with flash, emotion, or their gut feeling. There has to be substance, data, and logic. Be ready with all your information, and show K's you've got the facts.

The good news is that you only need to close the sale with one Knowledge type. Once you do, you can ask that person to be a reference for any other Knowledge types who want to investigate your products or services. They will help you close them, too, by sharing how they came to the conclusion that it was a smart decision to move forward with you. Close one Knowledge type, and more will logically follow.

EXERCISE

Memorize the twelve Knowledge values and become fluent in the Knowledge language.

Identify five things you can do to communicate and negotiate more effectively, and close more sales with a Knowledge type:

1. ______________________________

2. ______________________________

3. ______________________________

4. ______________________________

5. ______________________________

NOTES

CHAPTER 14

WHAT'S YOUR CODE?

"If people differ systematically in what they perceive and in how they reach conclusions, then it is only reasonable for them to differ correspondingly in their interests, reactions, values, motivations and skills."

— Isabel Briggs Meyers

In the last section, you learned a lot more about the four different types in the B.A.N.K. system. Which type do you identify most with? Blueprint? Action? Nurturing? Knowledge? Do you identify with just one type, or all four? While you may resonate with one type more than another, you likely connect to different aspects of all four types, creating what I call your full B.A.N.K. code.

Just like you don't fall into a single category, your prospects and customers are not just one of the four types either. They are also a combination of all four—which means they each also have a B.A.N.K. code.

The best analogy I can give you to explain a B.A.N.K. code is to compare it to your debit card. If you were to put your debit card into a local ATM machine, you would be required to enter your PIN code. Your PIN code is four digits, and you must enter that code in its exact sequence if you want money to come out. If you enter your PIN code in the wrong sequence, you will get an error message and need to try again. If you do it wrong more than a few times, the machine will reject your card, or even worse, confiscate it—at which point you'll be left with no money and no card.

If you deliver your presentation out of sequence, your customer will push back. You'll get an error message instead of cash—and you'll find yourself rejected and empty-handed, chalking it up as a *numbers game.*

Your customers are the exact same way! Instead of PIN codes, they have B.A.N.K. codes. You need to deliver your presentation customized exactly according to each person's full B.A.N.K. code if you want money to come out—or if you want to close the sale and get paid!

@CheriTree #WhyTheyBuy

CHOOSING THE RIGHT B.A.N.K. CODE SEQUENCE

Since every B.A.N.K. code is a combination of all four types, that means there are twenty-four different sequences or B.A.N.K. codes. While there are six combinations of codes for each primary type, the sequence of the code creates a very different combination, requiring a completely different approach. (We'll look at all twenty-four combinations shortly.)

Many salespeople make the mistake of thinking that if they can identify their prospect's primary type, they're all set and don't need anything else. Unfortunately, this blind spot is likely costing you a fortune in lost revenue.

After all, a person's secondary type matters a lot when it comes to presenting a message that best serves his or her inherent values. The secondary values temper primary values, lessening the impact of some and redirecting others. An A, for example, is always looking for a new opportunity for major success, but her secondary type tempers that drive to win.

An AN isn't going to be interested if the opportunity you're selling hurts others or the environment; he wants to find a big opportunity that helps other people as it creates the good life. An AB isn't going to be interested if the opportunity doesn't offer a simple system to get to the goal; she wants to find an opportunity with a solid structure to succeed already in place. An AK isn't going to be interested if the opportunity isn't backed up by objective facts; he wants to find an opportunity that is supported by science and logic. Your secondary type influences your values less than your primary type, but it has an impact.

The fourth and final type is even more important than someone's secondary type. After all, the final position represents the code your prospect identifies with least—or even a code that turns him or her off entirely. If you focus too heavily on that least important code by addressing that code's concerns, emphasizing its triggers, or featuring its primary values, you risk boring your prospect or, worse, hitting a tripwire that makes the sale impossible to close. Keeping a person's last code from the forefront of the conversation isn't just a good idea—it's vital to successful communication.

Let's look at the impact of the full code in action. Someone who has a B.A.N.K. code of Blueprint, Action, Nurturing, Knowledge (BANK) is very different from someone who is Blueprint, Knowledge, Nurturing, Action (BKNA). While both will need to learn about the system for success and want to get to the bottom line, the other codes dramatically impact why they buy. The BANK will want to know how the offer gets game-changing results and won't want to waste time looking at all the data piece by piece before making a decision. The BKNA won't be able to make a decision without the opportunity to inspect the data, and he or she will look at any perceived exaggeration much more harshly.

If you assumed that just because the BANK and BKNA are both Blueprints, you can deliver your presentation the same way, you'd be sadly mistaken. Since their values are in a different priority sequence, their buying motives are, too.

Unfortunately, in the sales world, when you're wrong—you don't get paid.

@CheriTree #WhyTheyBuy

When you understand people's full B.A.N.K. codes and apply the communication formulas we teach, you will innately deliver a presentation based in *why they buy*—and likely close the sale!

THE 24 B.A.N.K. CODES

BLUEPRINT	ACTION
B A N K	A B N K
B A K N	A B K N
B N A K	A N B K
B N K A	A N K B
B K N A	A K N B
B K A N	A K B N

NURTURING	KNOWLEDGE
N A B K	K A N B
N A K B	K A B N
N B A K	K N A B
N B K A	K N B A
N K B A	K B N A
N K A B	K B A N

Each code combination is unique and requires a different approach to get a yes instead of a no. At this point, it becomes obvious that it would be foolish to deliver the same presentation to every prospect—which explains why, as mentioned earlier, Salesforce.com says that 66 percent of customers feel turned off by a salesperson's presentation and why the Chally Group revealed that only 18 percent of buyers will buy from a salesperson who doesn't match the buyer's personality type, versus 82 percent when personality types are aligned.

THE ODDS

Now that you understand your prospect is one of these 24 codes, the math tells you that you have a 1 in 24 chance of delivering the right presentation—meaning you roughly have a 4 percent chance of delivering the right message—getting a yes—and a 96 percent chance of delivering the wrong message and getting a no.

Based on this, it makes sense that you've heard that sales is a numbers game—and the math tells us that the odds are definitely stacked against you. No wonder you've been told that in order to get more yeses, you have to get more nos!

So the question remains: How many chances will your prospect give you to deliver the right presentation? Just one.

@CheriTree #WhyTheyBuy

You cannot afford to risk your time, energy, or money in delivering the *wrong* presentation. You must deliver the correct one, every time. Your financial success depends on it!

HOW TO BEAT THE ODDS

At this point, there's only one good way to beat the odds, and that is to crack your prospect's code. Not knowing your prospect's B.A.N.K. code means you have to rely on your ability to wing it, speculate, assume, guess, or dance your way to the finish line—essentially, throwing spaghetti noodles against the wall and hoping they'll stick! As you learned in Section 1, sales is *not* an art without science, so you must know the science and the system of how to crack someone's code.

Although this book is all about understanding your prospect's B.A.N.K. code, it's equally important that you understand your own B.A.N.K. code. This will not only give you a powerful insight into understanding yourself, but it will also give you the perspective from which your prospects see you and how you need to adapt your approach accordingly to speak their language.

B.A.N.K. CODE ASSESSMENT

WHAT'S YOUR B.A.N.K. CODE?

So, after all this talk about B.A.N.K. codes, let's figure out what your own B.A.N.K. code is. The quickest way to do it is to use our proprietary technology, B.A.N.K. PASS, to crack your code in less than ninety seconds. This is a fast and easy way to determine your B.A.N.K. code.

Take a quick moment to crack your code online now. Go to mybankcode.com and enter the special Access Code located in the back of this book. This will unlock access to your customized B.A.N.K. Code Report at no cost and take you less than ninety seconds to complete. Once you've cracked your code online, record your code below.

MY B.A.N.K. CODE

Write down your B.A.N.K. code here.

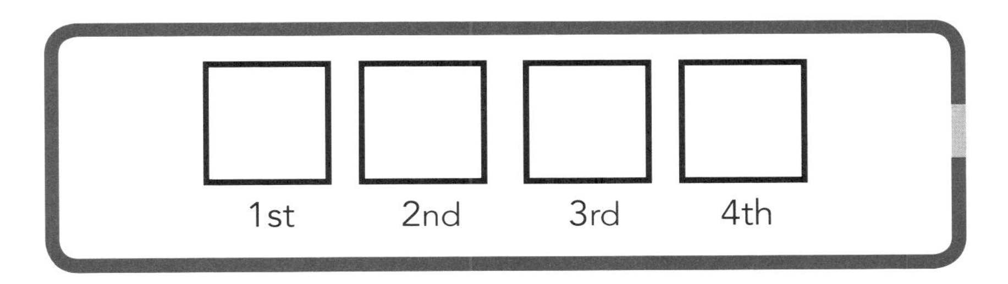

CHERI TREE'S B.A.N.K. CODE

Now that you know your B.A.N.K. code, I'll share my own code with you as well. Do you think you can guess it based on what you know so far? If you guessed ANKB, you guessed right! Here's my code:

- Action: 25 (I'm a very driven entrepreneur who looks for opportunity and takes massive action.)
- Nurturing: 23 (I love people and I'm passionate to make a difference in the world.)
- Knowledge: 22 (I like to learn new things, but I don't need to know everything before I take action.)
- Blueprint: 19 (I respect the need for systems and I know when to delegate.)

With our advanced assessments, available to our clients, there's a maximum high score of 25 in each category, and a minimum of 5, which reveals how weighted each part of your code is. This will give you more clarity and insight to your own B.A.N.K. code.

BEING DIVERGENT

Every blue moon, someone takes the Advanced B.A.N.K. Code Assessment and scores the same score on ALL four codes. While this is very rare, it's pretty cool to experience.

I've only seen this happen a few times, and the first time was when I met my business partner, Jenny Luetkemeyer. She attended one of my live B.A.N.K. training events in Southern California. During the course, we coded everyone and gave them each a nametag with their code on it, using colored stickers.

Throughout the entire course, she kept switching the order of her codes. It seemed like each time I taught about one of the codes, she would move that colored dot to her first position. She did that with all four codes. I could tell she was confused, as was I.

I was curious about why Jenny kept changing the order of her code. I'd never seen that before. We went to lunch and talked about it. She felt she could identify with each code, equally. We discussed it at great length, and she shared story after story that convinced me that each code was just as key as the other codes.

I then had her complete the Advanced Assessment and score herself. Sure enough, her scores were exactly the same, all the way across the board—she was divergent! This gave us both a lot of clarity and explained how she could shift gears so quickly from one code to another. Fascinating!

The more you practice connecting with each part of your code and your prospects codes, the more you will live a life that is in full color. Mastering the B.A.N.K. system has the power to transform your business and your life—and you can *take that to the bank*!

Regardless of your code, the key is to understand that every person is part Blueprint, Action, Nurturing, and Knowledge. You have all four types inside of you, and so does your prospect or key relationship.

@CheriTree #WhyTheyBuy

“There is no substitute for innovation. Original, revolutionary ideas will always rise to the top.”

— Richard Branson

SECTION 4: THE SOLUTION

In Section 3, I taught you the B.A.N.K. system and revealed the four B.A.N.K. types: Blueprint, Action, Nurturing, and Knowledge. Unfortunately, the B.A.N.K. system can't help you much unless you can easily figure out what types your prospects are and use the correct adaptive selling behaviors to close the sale, based on their underlying buying behavior.

When I was first developing B.A.N.K., finding this solution was the most challenging part for me. After all, it was not practical or even realistic that my prospect would take a fifty or one hundred question assessment prior to our appointment. I needed something much faster!

Experts have determined that you only have a few seconds to make a good first impression, and that first impression can make or break your sale. I couldn't afford to put my foot in my mouth by saying the wrong thing, ever. I needed to find a solution that would significantly increase my odds of closing the sale.

That's why I set about developing a coding solution that was fast, accurate, and simple enough that anyone could succeed. As a result, I created innovative tools, technology, and training that I desperately needed for increased sales. In this section, I'll reveal to you how to leverage each of these B.A.N.K. solutions for real results.

This section is all about delivering the ultimate solution—a way you can easily and accurately type your prospects in under ninety seconds every time. In addition to teaching you how to code any prospect successfully, I want to share stories of other B.A.N.K. users just like you so you can see what success with B.A.N.K. really looks like. As we wrap up this book, you'll come away with a step-by-step action plan for massive sales success.

B.A.N.K. transformed my life. Without the B.A.N.K. solution, I know I never would have achieved the life I am living today. I'd either still be stuck in the sales maytag with no way out or I'd simply have given up years ago. I want B.A.N.K. to deliver the same life-changing power to you. Learn the B.A.N.K. solution for sales success that you can *take to the bank*!

CHAPTER 15

CRACKING THE CODE

"The first and simplest emotion which we discover in the human mind is curiosity."

– Edmund Burke

Cracking your prospect's B.A.N.K. code is an essential part of making sure you deliver the right presentation, 100 percent of the time. The challenge is, how do you crack his or her code, and how do you make sure you get it right every time?

According to research, you only have seven seconds to make a good first impression. Your client is not going to give you much time in the exploration phase to figure him or her out, and you've only got one shot to get it right. You can try to ask great questions, listen for responses, make assumptions, and do your best to guess, but you can see by now that this will likely lead to getting a no instead of a yes.

The risk occurs when you try to wing it. Up to this point, I had never seen a scientific approach applied to the sales process. Without a proven system, we leave our sales appointments to chance, which is why 87 percent of salespeople do not feel prepared for their appointments.

Sadly, the old-school way of selling is to "mirror and match" your prospects, in hopes of building rapport so you can close the sale. This is a very antiquated sales philosophy, and it takes a reactive, instead of proactive, approach.

The new innovative approach I was looking for was to find a way to take all the guesswork out of sales and be proactive instead of reactive. After all, time is money, so I wanted to find a way I could crack people's codes in less than ninety seconds.

HOW TO CRACK SOMEONE'S CODE

The only way to crack someone's B.A.N.K. code in less than ninety seconds is simply to ask the person for his or her code. Unfortunately, once I had this realization, it was still a new concept, so I didn't know how to go about it—it wasn't like asking someone for his or her astrology sign. I had to find a more creative way to crack people's codes—and I did!

> **There's only one way to crack someone's code in such a small window of time–and get it right every time–you must ask your prospect for his or her code!**
>
> **@CheriTree #WhyTheyBuy**

I developed a set of four cards, with each card containing the values of its respective type. I then developed a systematic and scientific way to ask my prospect to sort the cards and determine his or her code.

This process was genius! It worked every single time! For the past two decades, 100 percent of the people I have asked to do this exercise have done it. Not one person has ever refused! Here's why:

1. People's curiosity gets the best of them.

2. The topic on the cards is about them—their favorite subject!
3. I use personality science to ask them to do the process with me.

When I started this process with my clients, I didn't even know whether it would work! It was simply an experiment. But the logic seemed plausible enough that it just made common sense that my prospect likely made buying decisions based on his or her code, and therefore, I needed a simple and fast way to crack that code!

THE PROCESS

Let me break it down for you. Here's how you can use personality science to crack someone's code:

Step 1. Hand your prospect the set of B.A.N.K. cards and ask him or her to do you a favor before you get started with your presentation. (Remember, Tony Robbins said, "Let your prospect determine your presentation." That means you need to know the prospect's code before you begin.)

Step 2. Ask your prospect to read the information on the cards. Each card has the top twelve values for its own type. (This part of the exercise is tapping into the Knowledge part of your prospect's B.A.N.K. code because he or she is reading information and learning.)

Step 3. Instruct your prospect to sort the cards in order, based on his top priority card to lowest priority card. Put the card that's most important and like him on top, down to least important and not like him on the bottom. (This part of the exercise is tapping into the Blueprint part of your prospect's B.A.N.K. code because you're giving him instructions, rules, and processes for the activity.)

Step 4. Tell your prospect that this process will help you serve him better. (This part of the exercise is tapping into the Nurturing part of your prospect's B.A.N.K. code because you are building a relationship with him and getting to know him better.)

Step 5. Tell him that this will also save you both some time. (This part of the exercise is tapping into the Action part of your prospect's B.A.N.K. code because he wants to hurry up and get to the bottom line! Plus, it's all about him.)

HOW TO EXPLAIN YOUR RATIONALE TO YOUR CLIENT

Occasionally, your prospect will ask you why you're doing this exercise with him or her. Here's how I explain it:

"Mr./Mrs. Prospect, the reason I've asked you to do this exercise with me is because I've found that this process allows me to serve you better and save us both some time. As you may have noticed, the title on each card says 'values.' By sorting the cards according to your values, it allows me to deliver a custom presentation based on what's most important to you, rather than delivering a presentation based on my assumptions of what I think is important to you."

Now what do you think happens automatically when you explain this process with your prospect? His respect for you goes up! Think about it; when was the last time a salesperson took the time to customize his presentation based on your prospect's exact value sets? Probably never. Therefore, your prospect feels much more comfortable moving forward with you.

This process allows you to be transparent and avoid the costly mistake of being ignorant or arrogant.

@CheriTree #WhyTheyBuy

Now you can confidently deliver your presentation based on what's most important to your customer, dramatically increasing the likelihood that he or she will want to do business with you.

B.A.N.K. CARD SUCCESS STORY

A few years ago, I met a man named Darren Goonawardana at one of my speaking engagements. He purchased our two-day live training course and got a set of the B.A.N.K. value cards. A few weeks later, he called to tell me he didn't think the cards would work with his business model. He was in high-end software sales to large B2B enterprise companies.

Darren told me his next appointment was with a billion-dollar company. He was meeting with the C-suite executives and board of directors to offer them his software solutions. He was competing with other companies and only had one shot to deliver his presentation to this group. He was nervous about using the cards in this environment and was basically calling to talk his way out of using them.

I reminded him that he only had one shot to deliver the right presentation, so why would he risk delivering the wrong presentation? He agreed. I trained him exactly on how to crack the code of the executive team and board members and told him he had nothing to lose, except the deal.

After the presentation, he called me to share what had happened. To his surprise, every member of the team cracked his or her code. He said they loved the activity! Not only was it fun, but it was competitive. Each team member wanted to know the codes of his or her peers. This was a great ice breaker that set Darren apart from his competition. But that's not the best part....

The best part for Darren was actually knowing his prospects' codes! Darren had made some assumptions in preparation for this big day. Because he was selling sophisticated software systems, he assumed the group would be weighted toward the Knowledge type. He also assumed that because he was talking to the C-suite executives, they were likely Blueprint and Action types.

To Darren's surprise, the dominant card of the group turned out to be Nurturing! This caught him so off guard that he realized he had prepared the wrong presentation that day. Because of his training with B.A.N.K., he knew the importance of delivering the right presentation, based on his prospects' B.A.N.K. codes. He then turned off the projector, closed his laptop, and delivered a completely different presentation, based on our specific scripting formulas...and it worked!

A few weeks later, Darren called me back to celebrate. He had closed a $250,000 deal, and he thanked me profusely for this game-changing training! He admitted that he never would have closed the deal had he not taken the B.A.N.K. training and cracked his prospects' codes in the boardroom.

BUILDING YOUR OWN B.A.N.K. SUCCESS

Darren is just one of countless thousands of clients around the world who are benefiting from the B.A.N.K. system—and you can be one too. Simply cracking the code before every sales call can bring you thousands, even millions, of dollars in additional income. It may feel intimidating to use the cards at first, but the cost of not asking for your prospect's code should scare you much more.

B.A.N.K. not only shares valuable information on how to close with your prospect, but it also sets you apart from the competition. Your prospect sees that you care deeply about serving his needs, so he connects better with your message. B.A.N.K. empowers you to crush the competition through superior customer service and communication. It truly is a game-changer!

NOTE: Only four or five cases have been reported back to me where an individual in a group setting has been asked to crack his or her code and refused. In each case, the individual later revealed the code in private and was either a Blueprint or Knowledge type. These two types tend to be more skeptical by nature. If you ever experience someone refusing to crack his or her code, you can likely deduce that the person is a high B or K—giving you the information you were looking for in the first place!

Either way, you win!

CHAPTER 16

FORENSIC B.A.N.K.ING

"When you have eliminated the impossible, whatever remains, however improbable, must be the truth."

– Sherlock Holmes

How much could you increase your sales numbers if you knew how to reveal your prospects' B.A.N.K. codes without even asking them? After all, sometimes it's just not possible to use B.A.N.K. cards. Maybe you're only communicating over the phone. Maybe the situation calls for a formal pitch where there isn't the flexibility to add a B.A.N.K. icebreaker. Maybe you need your presentation ready after only researching your prospect online or before ever meeting in person. Maybe you simply don't have your cards on you. (Although, I highly recommend you always keep at least one set with you).

In these cases, you've got to get into what I call forensic B.A.N.K.ing—figuring out someone's code accurately even though you haven't asked him or her directly. Luckily, two advanced techniques will help you crack someone's code and then apply what you've learned to your script.

SPEED CODING

Imagine having the detective skills of Sherlock Holmes. He is known for his amazing proficiency with observation, forensic science, and logical reasoning. Sherlock Holmes could take a quick look at your prospect and, after a short chat, know everything about her. While B.A.N.K. may not be able to help you solve most complex mysteries, you can use Holmes' exact skill set and our Speed Coding technique to deduce the code of your prospect in less than three minutes—and solve the valuable mystery of why she buys!

Speed Coding teaches you how to identify your prospect's buying behavior accurately without the use of the B.A.N.K. cards or the B.A.N.K. PASS (our online coding technology, which stands for Personality Assessment Success System). This technique takes your baseline knowledge and understanding of the B.A.N.K. system to the next level. While I can't teach you the entire strategy here, I want to give you the basics so you have an idea of how it's done and can start learning this valuable concept.

The three keys to Speed Coding are:

1. The power of observation
2. The art of questioning
3. Listening for clues

You use visual recognition clues, auditory triggers, and brief strategic introductory conversations to crack your prospect's code in the first three minutes after meeting her. Essentially, you use everything from the way she looks and acts to the way she answers specific get-to-know-you questions to deduce personality traits that correlate with the twelve key values of each type. Once you've got your mental list of values, you can put her B.A.N.K. code in the right order.

Just as Sherlock Holmes uses his special skills to solve mysteries, I use Speed Coding to crack codes.

@CheriTree #WhyTheyBuy

It's a powerful way to crack someone's code when you haven't even met the person yet. Speed Coding is great to use during conversations with prospects over the phone, where you can ask them questions and listen to their responses. You can also use Speed Coding to decipher a prospect's code by reviewing his or her presence online through social media profiles and website bios.

Speed Coding is so accurate that I've had people ask me whether I'm an FBI profiler! Nope! I'm just really good at knowing exactly what to look for and listen to with each person—and so are the clients I train on this technique.

I didn't develop these skills overnight, though. I practiced Speed Coding over and over for years. In fact, I'm a bit jealous of people learning Speed Coding now. The BANKCODE virtual simulations available on our Virtual Training (VT) platform have allowed students to become masters much more quickly—and without the embarrassment of miscoding an actual prospect and losing the sale!

I recently closed a major deal as a result of Speed Coding the CEO of a large company online. His Facebook ad showed up on my newsfeed, so I clicked through to his profile. As luck would have it, his company was on my target market list as a significant account to which I wanted to sell B.A.N.K. trainings. I spent less than ten minutes on his Facebook profile and the company's Fan page, and then I jumped over to his company website and LinkedIn profile page.

After investing about twenty-five minutes reviewing his company and personal profiles, I was able to craft a personalized message based on the B.A.N.K. code I deduced was his. I knew I only had one shot to make that first impression, so it had to be accurate.

POWER SCRIPTING

As you can imagine, simply knowing the CEO's code wasn't enough. I had to craft the perfect message to appeal to his code. That's when I turned to another Forensic B.A.N.K.ing technique: Power Scripting.

While any knowledge of B.A.N.K. is enough to connect with a person's values during an interpersonal interaction with him or her, you quickly have to distill your core value proposition into the person's B.A.N.K. code for a written message, speech, formal presentation, or elevator pitch. Power Scripting gives you the exact communication formulas you can use to communicate, negotiate, and close the sale, all based on a prospect's B.A.N.K. code.

You see, a key definition of the word script is "words in a sequence that have meaning." The definition of a Power Script, in our case, is "words in a sequence that have meaning to a particular code." The sequence matters in Power Scripting, as do the words you choose.

So how did I come up with these communication formulas? I developed the Power Scripting technique using another proven ancient teaching, this time developed by Aristotle, called the Rhetorical Triangle. Aristotle developed the Rhetorical Triangle formula to maximize influence and charisma, based on Ethos (credibility), Pathos (emotion), and Logos (logic). His formula has proven extremely powerful when applied in both the written and spoken word, and it forms the basis of top advice for persuasive communication available today.

I took Aristotle's rhetoric to a whole new level by applying B.A.N.K. principles to it. Essentially, I tapped into the parts of each message that appeal to each of the four codes in this three-part structure, and then I offered the right words to convince each code within this framework. Let's take a deeper look at why each part of the Rhetorical Triangle matters in B.A.N.K. language:

1. Ethos = Credibility. This means this part of your message will resonate with the Blueprint part of your prospect's code.
2. Pathos = Emotion. This means this part of your message will connect with the Action (excitement, intense emotion) and Nurturing (softer, heart-based emotion) parts of your prospect's code.
3. Logos = Logic. This means your message will make sense to satisfy the Knowledge part of your prospect's code.

You then can refocus on what matters most in your script based on your prospect's code.

FORENSIC B.A.N.K.ING SUCCESS STORY

Now that I knew the CEO's code, thanks to Speed Coding, I could use Power Scripting to ensure my quick Facebook message would resonate with him. Therefore, I wrote a script highly specific to his B.A.N.K. code using the right communication formulas, knowing that would increase the probability that he would not only read my message, but also respond favorably.

Speed Coding revealed his primary code was Action, so I kept it short and sweet and played to his ego. I briefly told him who I was and what I did, but most importantly, what was in it for him if he aligned with my company. I shared that our B.A.N.K. system would give him a considerable market advantage and be a key differentiator from his competition, which predominantly used the DiSC assessment instead. His second code was knowledge, so I made sure to add a dose of K to the script as well.

Here's the exact message I sent, with a few edits to keep his information private:

> Hi John,
>
> I'm Cheri Tree and I heard we need to meet! I just moved to Laguna Beach. I invented a system called B.A.N.K.™ which is designed to increase sales conversions and negotiations. We just completed a study at SFSU and are getting ready to publish a white paper where we were able to prove scientifically that B.A.N.K.™ could predict buying behavior and increase sales! It's a huge deal, and I would love to see if it's a good fit for you and your group. We were going to approach [your competition] but heard through the grapevine you're way more cool to work with! Let me know if you're open or would like to meet! People in your industry love it and it makes them "BANK"! Would love to hear back from you. Congrats on your success!

My Power Scripted message to him hit the bullseye! Notice how I complimented him and fed his ego (A), highlighted how this could help him crush his competition (A), validated that I'm not some crazy stalker on Facebook by adding the fact that we were getting a white paper published by San Francisco State University (K), then ended with how he could profit from this and one last stroke of the ego (A). Since N and B were the last two parts of his code, I left those parts off completely in this case. The AK combination needs it short, sweet, to the point and backed by logic.

He responded back to me with a very short message (again, very A!), telling me he liked the concept and to contact his Vice President of Business Development to discuss the proposed strategy. Within one week, I was in their corporate offices. Over the next few meetings, we formulated a game plan that would yield my company over a million dollars in revenue. What a way to take it to the BANK!

Forensic B.A.N.K.ing made it possible. I know I'd have never gotten that opening without both Speed Coding and Power Scripting to get my foot in the door. Sure, asking for a person's code is great, but in cases like this one, it's useless unless you get that first meeting—which online may already be too late.

Before we move on, here's another success story that shows Power Scripting works.

SUCCESS STORY – STEPHANIE B.

As a high Action, I've been known to wing it during prospect conversations and go with my gut feeling. Every conversation is an adventure. What challenges will arise this time? What dreams will be shared with me that I will have the privilege to support? I've been a singer and a stage performer my whole life, and I've been a voice coach for over twenty years. I find my clients primarily through word-of-mouth, and I've had times in my business when my practice is completely full.

But even as successful as I've been, I've had my share of missteps along the way. It's frustrating to see someone with big dreams decide to play it small and turn away from assistance I know could help change his or her life. After experiencing one of those particularly painful conversations, and on the cusp of a cycle in my business where I was experiencing some turnover, I decided to sit down and really evaluate what was happening.

It occurred to me that I wasn't consciously incorporating my B.A.N.K. training into my prospect conversations. I coded my prospects before our conversations. I was trained, licensed, and certified to teach B.A.N.K. Yet I was still going into conversations with the feeling that I could just handle whatever came my way. I had seven slots in my business I wanted to fill in the next thirty days, so I got serious. I sat down and used my Power Scripting skills not only to write out why each code would want to buy my services, but his or her potential objections and how I would respond to those objections.

Then, call by call, I had those scripts sitting in front of me. As the conversation progressed, I used them like Cliff Notes to remind myself how to shift between my prospects' languages. I was flexible and always listening to what my prospects had to say so I could respond to how they progressed through their codes. The first conversation ended in a yes, then the second, then the third.

By the end of the month, I'd had seven conversations and received seven yeses. My practice was once again full. I marveled at my 100 percent conversion rate for the month. My husband was thrilled that I had brought in over $10,000 right at the holidays. The best part was how wonderful it felt to have met my goal and ended the year on a high note. My success continued right into the new year. I brought in $50,000 in the first three months of 2017—my best start to a year ever.

One thing Cheri Tree has taught me is that knowing my code isn't an excuse for bad behavior. Even though I know I'm an Action, that doesn't give me an excuse not to have a strong plan and strategy when I'm speaking to prospects. What I love about B.A.N.K. is how much I've learned about myself and where I can be working to create more balance. My Blueprint husband also appreciates the changes he's seen in me, and it feels good for both of us to know that my business is taking off this year like never before.

IS LEARNING FORENSIC B.A.N.K.ING WORTH IT FOR YOU?

So do you need Forensic B.A.N.K.ing? Absolutely! These advanced B.A.N.K. strategies transform your skills from a B.A.N.K. novice to a B.A.N.K. expert—one who quickly and constantly closes deals.

The challenge for many salespeople is that they are trained to deliver their one particular script, but that script lacks meaning to most of their prospects because it fails to cater to their B.A.N.K. codes. Power Scripting intentionally communicates in the language of your prospect, dramatically increasing the chances of getting a yes and closing the sale. Speed Coding makes this possible before you've ever met the person face-to-face.

Forensic B.A.N.K.ing provides an absolutely essential skill set that you must master if you want to succeed like the super-achievers.

@CheriTree #WhyTheyBuy

The key to fast tracking your success is to use Speed Coding to crack your prospect's code, followed by Power Scripting techniques so you always speak or write the messages that will trigger your prospect to buy. I developed very specific formulas and techniques to follow to give me the highest probability of closing the sale. I encourage you to learn these techniques so you, too, can experience the benefits of B.A.N.K.ING with your prospects and key relationships.

Identify five ways you can apply Speed Coding techniques in your business:

1. ______________________________
2. ______________________________
3. ______________________________
4. ______________________________
5. ______________________________

Identify five ways your sales scripts need to be altered using Power Scripting techniques:

1. ______________________________
2. ______________________________
3. ______________________________
4. ______________________________
5. ______________________________

Before we leave this topic, here's a testimonial that the B.A.N.K. personality system works.

SUCCESS STORY – JILL M.

I know the B.A.N.K. personality system works because I put it to the test and it passed with flying colors! Let me back up a bit and tell you my success story: After I went through all the training to become a certified and licensed B.A.N.K. trainer, I wanted to test it for myself. I mean, I knew it made sense on paper and that I could teach this incredible system to others, but could it really make a difference in my own sales career? I had an annual sales quota to hit for the fiscal year beginning on July 1.

So...I decided to use the B.A.N.K. cards and the Speed Coding techniques I had learned to see whether I could increase my sales by 300 percent in 90 days (I like the personal challenge). At the time, I was selling print advertising space for a publication. With each customer that I currently had (I wanted the renewal business from them), I speed coded them and pitched to them in their dominant "buying" language focusing on the triggers and staying away from the tripwires. I got 100 percent of their business. For the new customers, I used the B.A.N.K. cards in most cases and some I used the Speed Coding technique. I started my quest on July 19, and by Aug 12, I had surpassed my sales quota by 4 percent. That's right....in less than 30 days, I was at 104 percent of my annual income goal, with signed contracts. So when people dare to ask me whether B.A.N.K. works, I confidently tell them, "Yes, it does! I tested it for myself."

NOW WHAT?

Now that you know how to determine your prospects' B.A.N.K. codes and how to Power Script messages to them, you're ready to close the deal and enjoy success, right? But wait—there's more. We'll connect some more dots in the next chapter to ensure your success.

CHAPTER 17

CONNECTING THE DOTS

"I'm not telling you it's going to be easy. I'm telling you it's going to be worth it."

– Art Williams

When I taught B.A.N.K. at Harvard University, I learned a very important question the graduate students have to answer when they do their dissertations:

"So what, now what?"

@CheriTree #WhyTheyBuy

"So what, now what?" is exactly what you should be asking yourself right now. How do you apply these concepts to let your prospect determine your presentation? How can this information alter your marketing materials, website, email campaigns, sales presentations, inter-office dynamics, leadership teams, hiring processes, and your entire life, so you can take it to the bank?

CODE EVERYONE, EVERYWHERE

The best way to make a difference with B.A.N.K. is to code everyone, everywhere. Take advantage of every opportunity to crack the code of each person you know. This information is valuable and can help you better communicate, collaborate, negotiate, and close the sale faster. Whether you use the B.A.N.K. value cards in-person for a basic understanding of others or B.A.N.K. PASS, our online coding tool, to get a custom detailed report on your prospect, you'll know the best way to get your message across.

I personally always code everyone I meet. I find it helps foster communication. Here are just a few strategies you can use to code everyone.

AT NETWORKING EVENTS

Networking events are all about connecting with others quickly. B.A.N.K. gives you the tools you need to create deeper bonds even in the brief moment when you get to talk to each new connection.

- Bring your B.A.N.K. value cards to every networking event. This is a great icebreaker when you're meeting new people; most people find it a fun alternative to the same old small talk. Plus, you can quickly determine how to approach your conversation with them and take the next step.
- Offer to send them a free report using your B.A.N.K. PASS subscription as a free gift. This is always a great incentive to secure an email, so you can put them in a funnel.
- When you collect their business cards, you can write their codes directly on them. I recommend you go to the local office supply store and buy the little colored sticker dots to put on the cards when you're back at your office. This will remind you what each person's B.A.N.K. code is at a glance.
- Take a picture of your prospect holding up his or her B.A.N.K. code with the cards and store it in your phone as a profile picture of the person. Every time she calls you, you'll have her code on your screen, reminding you how to communicate. You can also store her code in your phone with her name so you won't forget it.

AT THE REGISTRATION TABLE

Use B.A.N.K. to set the right tone at your conferences or events by integrating it into the registration process. You'll be able to communicate with attendees effectively from the very first moment they arrive.

- When you host your own events, have several sets of B.A.N.K. cards at the registration table. When your guest signs in, ask him to crack his code and write it down on the registration form.
- Put the colored dots on his nametag in the order of his B.A.N.K. code. This will allow you to communicate with him accordingly. It also helps the speaker connect better with the audience, and it helps the sales teams at your event know how to close better because the customer is wearing his code on his nametag.
- Offer to send each person a customized B.A.N.K. Code Report with your B.A.N.K. PASS subscription. This also makes sure that you electronically capture every person's code in your online dashboard.

NOTE: If you're using an online registration system, integrate your B.A.N.K. PASS link in the registration process so you can capture every guest's B.A.N.K. code even before the day of the event and use that knowledge to communicate better during the buildup to the big day.

OVER THE PHONE

Communication has even more pitfalls on the phone. You can't see people's body language to gauge their responses to what you're saying, so you need to know definitively that you're using the right words.

- It's important that you know someone's code, even while you're talking to him on the phone. You can code on the spot—or even before you ever pick up the phone.
- You may not be able to use B.A.N.K. cards without a face-to-face meeting, but you can still crack someone's code over the phone by applying our B.A.N.K. Speed Coding techniques. These can be learned by attending our live or virtual Speed Coding course.
- Use your B.A.N.K. PASS subscription and ask your prospect to take ninety seconds and crack his code before the call. Remind him that this will help you serve him better and save you both some time. You'll get the results sent to you immediately, and now you'll have the right way to approach them during your call.

ON THE INTERNET

The Internet has become the best way to research your prospect before a big meeting. Since 87 percent of sales professionals don't feel prepared for their appointments, cracking a person's code using the Internet can make all the difference in being properly prepped.

- If you're preparing to meet with a very important prospect or gatekeeper, you absolutely must crack his code in advance of your appointment. Speed Coding can be used to crack someone's code online through social media profiles, including Facebook and LinkedIn.
- You can include your B.A.N.K. PASS link in your email signature so anyone you email has access to your link. Include a line informing your correspondents that they can crack their codes to get a free customized B.A.N.K. Code Report.
- You can put your link on your website and opt-in forms so you capture their info as they opt-in to your database. This will give you very valuable data on whom your online leads are and how to approach them.

DURING MARKETING CAMPAIGNS

Internet marketing campaigns generate an average of 760 percent more revenue when they are segmented effectively and personalized to the recipients. Segmenting your marketing materials by B.A.N.K. code makes lead generation efforts and sales funnels more effective.

- Post your B.A.N.K. PASS subscription link online in many different groups and forums as a way to generate a lead. After all, how powerful would it be if you could generate a lead *and* know the person's B.A.N.K. code? Offering a free B.A.N.K. Code Report to your customers and prospects is a great value proposition and a way to generate a lot more leads online.

- BANKIFY your online sales funnel. Rather than sending all your online traffic to a one-size-fits-all sales funnel, imagine cracking the code of your prospective leads, and then redirecting them to the landing pages and sales funnels based on their B.A.N.K. codes. This will take your online sales conversion to the next level.
- You can apply this BANKIFICATION technique to all your marketing materials, websites, brochures, landing pages, auto-responder campaigns, newsletters, and more.
- Specifically communicate and sell to your prospects in customized ways, based on their B.A.N.K. codes, instead of using a cookie-cutter approach. Click-through rates skyrocket when the content in the message speaks to a person's code.

SUCCESS STORY

Some of our clients have generated more than 100 leads in less than one hour just by posting their links in various online groups. This is much less expensive than paying for leads and you get their B.A.N.K. codes included!

IN YOUR CRM DATABASE

Your CRM is a vital way to keep track of all your prospects and clients in today's Internet-based economy. BANK-ifying your CRM amps up its power and makes it easier to communicate with every person in the database.

- With your B.A.N.K. PASS subscription, you get access to your online dashboard, which reveals every prospect that has cracked his or her code with your subscription link. You can gain valuable insight about the codes in your database, simply by logging into our platform.
- You can also download the data and export all the codes, based on personality type categories. You can take that data, upload it into your existing CRM platform, and build different email lists, based on the dominant codes of your database. Now you can communicate to your own email list differently, by segmenting your list based on B.A.N.K. codes.
- If you are a larger enterprise client, we can do an API integration with the data inside your corporate B.A.N.K. PASS dashboard and pull the codes straight into your existing CRM platform. This integration will allow everyone on your internal teams to know how to communicate and negotiate more effectively, and close sales consistently. It can also help increase retention and improve customer satisfaction scores.

WITHIN YOUR TEAM

Communicating effectively in the workplace can not only improve teamwork but even make your company exponentially more productive.

- Use the B.A.N.K. system to code your sales force, employees, independent contractors, downline sales organization, franchisees, customers, patients, clients, team members, and more.
- Display their B.A.N.K. codes in their offices, on their business cards, on their name plates, employee badges, etc. This is a fun way to incorporate B.A.N.K. into your entire culture, and it will significantly improve internal communication and teamwork.

IN YOUR PERSONAL RELATIONSHIPS

Nothing matters more than our loved ones, but sometimes we struggle to communicate with the people who matter most to us. B.A.N.K. can change that by improving communication outside of work, as well.

- B.A.N.K. transcends your professional life because it can also significantly improve your personal life. Coding friends and family is a fun activity that will shift the way you interact with each person, once you know his or her code.
- It's a good idea to code your spouse, partner, children, family members, and friends. This will give you tremendous insight into how to interact with each of them based on their codes.

SUCCESS STORY

I've had countless people tell me how B.A.N.K. has saved their marriage, made them a better parent, and deepened friendships. B.A.N.K. even helped a friend prevent a teenage suicide. These success stories have been so powerful that we developed a B.A.N.K. course for relationships, which is significantly impacting the lives of families all around the world.

AMONG THE SCHOOL STAFF

Your children deserve the best education possible. This depends on excellent communication between your child, the school staff, and yourself. B.A.N.K. makes that communication infinitely easier.

- If you have children in school, it's a good idea to code the teachers and staff at the school, in addition to your children. Then you'll know the best way to communicate your child's needs and your concerns so nothing important is missed.
- It's also a good idea to have a meeting with the teachers to share your child's code. This can help the teacher adjust the way he or she teaches and interacts with your child.
- We have designed the B.A.N.K. value cards for children as well, so you can use the cards with younger people.

NOTE: Although I'm not a psychologist or psychiatrist, it's possible that little Johnny is not A.D.H.D. He may simply be an Action type with ants in his pants who's being taught by a teacher with a different code. Something to think about.... I'd love to see B.A.N.K. help our education system serve our children better!

B.A.N.K. CASE STUDIES

Of course, you don't have to take my word for it that these B.A.N.K. strategies deliver results. Let our success stories guide you. Over the past several years, we've gathered case studies from many different industry professionals who have applied the B.A.N.K. methodology to their business or practice. Here are a few of our favorite examples that may inspire you to apply B.A.N.K. to your own business.

HOW B.A.N.K. TRANSFORMED A SALES TEAM

Let's use my own story as our first case study. Once I realized the B.A.N.K. system's power, I wanted to implement this training into my entire sales organization. I organized a two-day live training event for 200 people. I taught them the B.A.N.K. system—specifically, how to close more sales and recruit more distributors.

We soon incorporated B.A.N.K. into every part of our business. We used B.A.N.K. at all our live guest sales events, cracking the codes at the registration table and putting the revealed codes on our guests' nametags. When our leaders did three-way calls with their prospects, we required them to tell us their prospect's B.A.N.K. code before we did the call.

It worked. Our sales results exploded! I had people who had never made $100,000 in a year prior to this training, earn $250,000, $500,000, and even over $1 million within one year. Once I trained my sales team on this system, my personal income broke a record in this industry that has still not been surpassed. I took my income from $8,000 to $261,000 in just twenty-eight days!

HOW B.A.N.K. TRANSFORMED A DENTAL PRACTICE

The primary dentist of a major dental practice became certified to train B.A.N.K. She taught her office staff and the entire dental team about the codes so they could interact with the patients differently, according to their codes. Patient care and satisfaction improved because patients felt their needs and concerns were better addressed.

In addition, the dentist's staff uses B.A.N.K. PASS to crack the code of every lead they generated online so they know the best way to sell their services to each prospective customer. They code every patient who walks in the door with the B.A.N.K. value cards and put the colored dots on the patient's medical file jacket so everyone knows the patient's code. They then offer additional services and treatments to the patients, based on their B.A.N.K. codes.

B.A.N.K. is even a tool used to communicate with the office staff and other dentists in the office, so there's better relationships and less conflict.

HOW B.A.N.K. TRANSFORMED A LAW PRACTICE

An attorney uses B.A.N.K. to code all of his prospective clients so he can not only win them as clients, but also improve his communication during their cases dramatically. This leads to more clients and a thriving legal practice.

B.A.N.K. hasn't just made the attorney's close rate when prospecting more successful, however. It's also improved his win rate in court. He uses his Speed Coding skills to crack the code of the opposing counsel. This helps him prepare his arguments based on the opposing counsel's code and anticipate his or her strategy based on common behavior patterns associated with that person's code. He also uses his Speed Coding skills to crack the judge's code so he can alter his defense to make the most progress for his case. He even uses B.A.N.K. to Speed Code the jury members. Every jury member has a different B.A.N.K. code, and knowing those codes, the attorney can change his strategy to win them over.

HOW B.A.N.K. TRANSFORMED A REAL ESTATE AGENCY

A successful realtor uses B.A.N.K. to code every one of her potential clients. She uses this information to prepare for appointments and to show them the right houses, based on their codes. As a result, they are more likely to buy, and more satisfied with their entire experience.

B.A.N.K. doesn't just make buyers happy. It improves the realtor's success with sellers, too. She uses B.A.N.K. to get listings from families selling their homes and alters her listing presentation based on their codes. She then uses B.A.N.K. to market and advertise for new clients, targeting specific marketing campaigns geared to the codes that would be most responsive to certain properties or neighborhoods.

She even uses the B.A.N.K. value cards as an icebreaker when she's hosting an open house. Every person attending gets to crack his or her code, and then she talks to the prospective buyers based on the revealed codes. Everyone feels included—which turns to feeling understood when their unique concerns about buying a home are addressed right away by the realtor.

SUCCESS STORY – JANE J.

I was reading a post on DISC on LinkedIn today and it struck me that the DISC profile is all about learning about yourself. I get that. The writer spoke of how we act influences how we behave. Five years ago, this was helpful to me in discovering my own strengths and weaknesses. However, in sales, if we speak only our own language and are communicating in a way that works for us, we become unidirectional: we don't listen to our clients and we don't connect well.

B.A.N.K. is a tool that allows us to discern how to communicate in a way our clients will listen to. It's simple and effective. It allows us to "read" our clients and interact with them in a way that is effective *for them.*

I took my first B.A.N.K. course a year and a half ago, and I quickly realized that by having my clients share their values with me and tell me how they want to be communicated with, I am way more "intuitive." My clients feel I "get them."

There has been a measurable result as well: After taking B.A.N.K. a year and a half ago, I increased my effectiveness in sales by closing 66 percent more transactions per year. This past year, I sold sixty-seven homes and received the REMAX Chairman's Award.

How did I do that? I used B.A.N.K. to ensure that my listing and buyer presentations reached all BANK personalities so I hit everyone's *hot* buttons. This allowed me to win more listing presentations and enlist more buyers.

I also used B.A.N.K. in my social media campaigns to generate more clients by tailoring specific posts for specific codes. I have market updates for Knowledge, step-by-step process videos for Blueprint, quick-paced live videos for Action types, and warm, fuzzy videos for Nurturers.

I am about to be on a TV show called *Seller's Market* in which I will compete with four other very successful realtors for listings. It's high stakes since we will only have ten minutes to convince the sellers to list with us. I attended the B.A.N.K. power scripting course specifically to research the personality types and develop my listing scripts so I can be very effective in a short period of time. The feedback was invaluable to me, specifically for the codes I don't relate to well. I am going into this show armed and ready for any type of seller.

HOW B.A.N.K. TRANSFORMED A PROPERTY MANAGEMENT COMPANY

A property manager uses B.A.N.K. not only to win new clients, but to retain existing accounts.

SUCCESS STORY – JULIE S.

Using B.A.N.K. has helped me close $29,465 per month in new accounts ($353k in one year). Our firm typically turns over 100 percent of our clients from year to year, so we have to earn them back. Using B.A.N.K., our second and beyond year(s), retention rate has risen to 80-plus percent. This has equated to $23,572 + each month in the second and future years of continued service. This is a sustained income of over $282,864 per year in the second year and beyond. Additionally, clients we have had for more than ten years feel we got a "pep in our step" as we began to speak their language all the time. They are happier than ever with our service.

I am thrilled to know the formula of the B.A.N.K. methodology, and all I can say is *it works*!

HOW B.A.N.K. TRANSFORMED A CONSULTING COMPANY

SUCCESS STORY – SHELLY P.

After a successful twenty-five-year business-to-business sales career, I didn't think there would be anything in the sales training world that could help me win more business. However, while attending a conference a couple of years ago, I was introduced to B.A.N.K. and was blown away. I can remember sitting in the audience with light bulbs going off left and right in my head and thinking back on a couple of prospects I hadn't closed in the past. I knew immediately which personality types those prospects had been and how I could adapt my sales pitch to give them what they needed to say yes. I went back to some of those contacts and closed many of them. I was able to prove for myself that B.A.N.K. works.

I realized B.A.N.K. is not only a revolutionary training system, but it is also a missing link in the sales process. I added B.A.N.K. as an integral part of my sales consulting and training program because I think every salesperson and business owner should know how to use this invaluable tool to win more business and provide better customer service.

Applying B.A.N.K. to my business has been amazing! I reduced my sales cycle 50 percent (from four months to two months) by identifying my prospect and staying in his or her B.A.N.K. code from my initial meeting through subsequent follow-ups and all the way through to close. I have been able to increase my fees and close the largest client in the history of my company since becoming an entrepreneur. I have also increased sales over 200 percent during the first quarter of 2017 compared to the first quarter of 2016.

On a personal note, I communicate more effectively with all of the personality types and build deeper relationships much more quickly. My spouse and I are both Blueprints and we love each other for it every day. Where was B.A.N.K. when my stepdaughter was a teenager? After learning B.A.N.K., we realized she was the Action type. That certainly answered a lot of questions that would have been nice to know many years ago.

There is truly nothing like B.A.N.K. in the marketplace. It is easy to learn, understand, and apply.

HOW B.A.N.K. TRANSFORMED A FINANCIAL ADVISOR'S BUSINESS

A financial advisor uses B.A.N.K. to code every client. This helps him to communicate better with his existing clients. Increased trust is the result—and that means that both the financial advisor and the client make more money.

He uses B.A.N.K. PASS to crack the code of prospective clients before having the first appointment. He tells them that this ninety-second exercise will help him prepare better for their appointments and save them both some time. Once he knows their codes, he puts together the right type of financial discussion and marketing materials. This helps him understand the best financial products to offer, investment strategies, risk tolerance levels, and other factors that will make a given client feel comfortable so he can make the best recommendations possible.

He also uses B.A.N.K. to follow up with his customers and prospects after determining how much information or time they need to take the next step. Once he determines their B.A.N.K. codes, he constantly reminds himself of their codes by putting the colored code sticker dots on each client file and their codes in his database. B.A.N.K. is integrated in the financial advisor's entire system so he always knows how to communicate best with his clients.

HOW B.A.N.K. IS TRANSFORMING THE WORLD

No matter your field or business, you can benefit from B.A.N.K. These case studies show just a small sample of the variety of professionals transforming their successes through B.A.N.K. I now have hundreds of top leaders using B.A.N.K. to grow their businesses explosively faster than ever before. We are even bringing this training into international companies at the corporate level so we can help the entire organization gain significant momentum and take it to the bank!

B.A.N.K. is transforming the way the world does business—one organization at a time.

@CheriTree #WhyTheyBuy

HOW YOU CAN USE B.A.N.K.

The applications of B.A.N.K. are endless—and the success stories we get on a daily basis are heartwarming and humbling. I've witnessed countless lives change as a result of using this powerful gift. B.A.N.K. is far more than a tool, system, or methodology—it's a way of life! I encourage you to use this tool on a daily basis, both at work and at home. It changed my life and the way I do business, and now it can change yours too! B.A.N.K. is a game-changer!

Entrepreneurs, sales professionals, business owners, direct sales professionals, network marketers, financial services experts, real estate agents, professional service providers, online marketers, relationship counselors, speakers, authors, coaches, business consultants, corporate salespeople, employees, leaders, executives, educators, non-profits, and thousands of other professionals can benefit from B.A.N.K. It's not just these people who can use B.A.N.K. for greater success, either. The list goes on and on. Most importantly, *you* can benefit from B.A.N.K.!

Start to integrate B.A.N.K. into everything your business does today. It's time to build your own B.A.N.K. success story.

Identify five ways you can apply B.A.N.K. to your current business practice to create better relationships with your customers, serve them better, and close more sales:

1. ______________________________

 ____

 ____

2. ______________________________

 ____

 ____

3. ______________________________

 ____

 ____

4. ______________________________

 ____

 ____

5. ______________________________

 ____

 ____

CHAPTER 18

INSIDE JOB

"I think every person has their own identity and beauty. Everyone being different is what is really beautiful. If we were all the same, it would be boring."

– Tila Tequila

Although I created the B.A.N.K. system for sales, I later realized that was just the tip of the iceberg. Beneath the surface, B.A.N.K. was impacting the core of every single relationship I had. It was not just a tool I could use on the outside, but a way of life that changed me on the inside.

Several years ago, I had the opportunity to crack my parents' codes. My mom is a BNAK and my dad is an ANKB (my same code). I had always assumed my mom was a Nurturing type, but once she revealed her code, I was able to connect the dots all the way back to my childhood and the way I was raised.

My mom is actually a Blueprint. It now made sense why I had to do my chores before I could go outside and play, or why I had to set the table the exact same way every time, or why we had a family planning meeting every Sunday evening so my mom could schedule all the different activities throughout the week. And now it made more sense why I had a curfew and when I didn't respect it, I was grounded. I thought rules were merely suggestions—apparently my mom didn't think that was too funny!

My dad, on the other hand, was an Action. No wonder he was a fighter pilot! He coached our sports teams, took us camping, went boogey boarding with us in the ocean, and bought a scooter for me to drive while I was still a teenager! My dad was easier to negotiate with too. I remember that if I wanted something "off the list" from the grocery store, I'd make sure I went shopping with my dad instead of my mom.

Knowing my family's B.A.N.K. codes suddenly gave meaning and understanding to every relationship and memory I had with them. I was able to understand why my brother Tim was a bookworm growing up—because he was a Knowledge! I understood why my brother Tom wanted to organize everything and why he got annoyed if I would move something to a different place in his bedroom. He was a Blueprint!

It was a magical experience for me to think back to every memory I had and now relive it through the filter of their B.A.N.K. codes. I was no longer frustrated that Tim wanted to read all the time instead of going out to play with me. I was no longer compelled to heckle my brother Tom by moving things around in his room. I understand and appreciated his need for order.

In one moment, by simply understanding each person's B.A.N.K. code, I was able to see my life in full color. My love and appreciation for each person grew instantly. At the same time, any hurts or resentments eroded away. I found myself having much greater empathy for every human being, and I released any preconceived judgments about them I had been quick to make.

B.A.N.K. has allowed me to fall in love with the entire human race! I now understand that we need a world with all four codes. God, in His infinite wisdom, created a planet with a mixture of all of us.

The Blueprint types bring order and structure to our world. From traffic lights to tax and legal systems, we are able to build an entire society and economy with their input. Without them, our world would operate in utter chaos.

The Action types bring an entrepreneurial spirit and an unrivaled excitement and enthusiasm for life. From sporting events to free enterprise, Actions keep our world moving forward and filled with entertainment. Without them, we would live in a very boring world.

The Nurturing types bring all the love we need to make this world a better place. They put the human into humanity and are on a relentless pursuit for utopia and world peace. Without them, we would likely destroy the entire human race.

Lastly, the Knowledge types bring incredible innovation and education—from the invention of the lightbulb, the automobile, and the telephone to computer systems and space travel. Without them, we'd be stuck back in the Stone Age.

B.A.N.K. was changing the entire way I saw the world, and each relationship that was a part of my world.

This is also true for my clients. Over the years, story after story after story has been told to me from my clients all over the world. They tell me how B.A.N.K. has saved their marriages, made them better parents, and allowed them to reconnect with people they had disconnected from because of personality differences.

Don't just take it from me. Here's a few stories of how B.A.N.K. has transformed the lives of countless people from around the world.

The fact is that B.A.N.K. is the most important language you could ever learn to speak! It's the Rosetta Stone for the human race, with the power to unlock the secrets to communicating in ways that you've never thought were possible.

@CheriTree #WhyTheyBuy

A MARRIAGE SAVED – SUZANNE M.

My marriage of nearly fifteen years has been a long, drawn-out miscommunication between a super Blueprint and a Divergent (equal in all four codes). You know what's almost as bad as a Post-it note breakup (à la Carrie Bradshaw in *Sex in the City*)? A conversation about divorce over text. Yep. Strangely enough, I wasn't the one who started it. Shocking. However, things were said that needed to be said.

To prepare for what awaited me at home, I spent some time crafting a script for speaking with husband, using the Blueprint dialect. Just by crafting the script, I gained a better understanding of how we ended up where we found ourselves, time and time again. It was a humbling moment. I realized how my actions had fueled the almost certainty of the destruction of our marriage, despite my strong desire and attempts to make it work.

Little did I know that our impending conversation weighed heavily on my husband's mind on Friday. He saw a couple in a seminar he was attending who could have been us. Two decent-looking people, working side by side...but not. No affinity between the two. A team in name only.

It dawned on him that they were a reflection of us. And he didn't want it to be that way. There's always been a Nurturer in him, but he didn't feel safe tapping into it with me. It was too risky. Until last night's conversation.

A few hours after my arrival home, I had a chance to sit down quietly with my husband. Our conversation didn't turn out the way it had in the past. I thought it would fall upon deaf ears once again. But, it didn't. Using Blueprint terminology and weaving it into a difficult conversation that expressed what was needed in our relationship to move forward resulted in a renewed understanding and trust between us—something that hasn't been there in a long time.

I'm happy to say we have renewed our commitment to be better partners to one another. He feels safe with me again, for the first time in fifteen years. And I finally understand the depth of his love and commitment to me. Over time, he'll learn the words (and behaviors) that work best for me, and I will continue to use the words and behaviors that make him feel safe. Our marriage and family have been spared—because of Power Scripting.

This week has been one of the most challenging, informative, and transformative weeks in my life. I want to thank each of you for providing the experience and education of a lifetime.

MORE COMPASSION – KIMCHI C.

B.A.N.K. helped me to have more compassion toward others who are not like me. It helped me connect more at their level, and be more present with them. It helped me get out of "my need for being right" and to be more humble and understanding. It has saved me from many heartaches and arguments with my family members. To me, this is an impact that I value and like to share with others.

COMMUNICATION IS THE THREAD OF LIFE – TRINA W.

The moment I met Cheri Tree and learned about BANKCODE, I knew my life would never be the same. The temperature in the room changed when she began to speak, and my response was so visceral that words still cannot do it justice. Being in the presence of a True Visionary and Authentic Leader changed me on a cellular level. I hung onto Cheri's every word and BANKCODE literally gave me the puzzle piece I'd longed for. Years of therapy and soul-searching never gave me the clarity that BANKCODE did in just ninety seconds! I was blown away!

Cracking the code to my unique life and understanding why I function the way I do gave me a sense of peace and self-forgiveness I had never felt before. In fact, it gave me a new understanding of my family, my friends, and humanity in general. My relationships began to change, my business expanded, and I decided to become a BANKCODE consultant! I want to share Cheri's genius all over the world because she's created a system that connects us all using one simple language.

Communication is the thread of life, and Cheri has given us an amazing tool to shift our relationships with each other and with those around us. BANKCODE is spreading like wildfire, and it's such an honor to be a part of the journey. World peace is upon us, and we now have the vehicle that will get us there. Thank you, Cheri, from the bottom of my heart.... I'm a BANKER for life!

IT IS NEVER TOO LATE - LINDA C.

B.A.N.K. has had a tremendous impact on my relationship with my mother. We both love each other very much, but ever since I can remember, I always felt impatient with her. Mom's need to tell me what to do or not to do always drove me crazy. I am a very high AN. I always "controlled" myself so as not to hurt her feelings. Turns out, she is a huge B, which is my last code (and a very low one).

Now equipped with the knowledge of B.A.N.K., I have found a new respect for my mother. I shared my B.A.N.K.

knowledge with her and we now enjoy discovering and relating at a different level. We have learned to embrace what separated us. Mom is now in her seventies, and I am so thankful to B.A.N.K. for enabling us to grow our relationship at this stage of our lives. It is never too late! No other personality-based system ever provided me with the key to understanding my mother's values. I feel so grateful!

NO MORE BULLYING – JEANIE C.

I'm so thankful for B.A.N.K. I have a program, Bully Proofing You, that I train all over the world. B.A.N.K. has not only helped me increase my sales of Bully Proofing You, but it has also given me the tools to help my clients better. B.A.N.K. has given me a language that all people can use to understand themselves and each other at a deeper level.

When Cheri Tree was training me on the B.A.N.K. system, I immediately saw the benefits for using it in conjunction with Bully Proofing You. The coding allows us all to have great comprehension when talking about behavior and why people react to things they do. It also gives people the keys to understanding themselves, which correlates to understanding others as well.

One of the reasons people bully others is pain. Bullies are in pain so they lash out. They are in reaction mode. It's not about the other person at all. It's 100 percent about them and what they are going through. However, as the person on the receiving end of that attack, it can seem very personal. By remembering we have the N-Nurturing code in us, we can respond appropriately. We can have compassion for the pain the other person is feeling. We can have empathy for the person instead of taking it personally.

No matter what your code is, B.A.N.K. will help you understand those you interact with on a deeper, more meaningful level. I have so many people who have let me know how Bully Proofing You and B.A.N.K. have changed their lives.

One family in particular comes to mind. They were having many problems. They couldn't get along. The constant bickering and lack of understanding had driven a wedge so deeply into their family that they all wanted to call it quits.

The husband and wife wanted a divorce. The two children didn't even want to be together or with either parent. It was a terrible mess. After they attended my three-day training, learned the B.A.N.K. system, and got some mentoring, I am proud to say they are a thriving happy family.

What was the issue? After coding them with B.A.N.K., we realized each member of the family had a totally different B.A.N.K. code. They didn't understand each other and why things were being done the way they were. Each person thought the others were broken or out to get him or her. They also each wondered whether he or she was the one who was not functioning well. Once they understood each other better, they could communicate and get to a common ground from which to build. B.A.N.K. and Bully Proofing You saved their family.

I also use B.A.N.K. with my teenage clients who are dealing with bullying. The dark side of bullying is missed potential and a higher risk for suicide. I recently had a parent contact me to thank me for giving him back his daughter. He no longer had to worry about her taking her life. When the daughter came to me, her personal value was so low because of the bully between her ears that she just wanted to end it all. "I just want the pain to stop and I don't care how," she said to me.

I coded her and her family. She was the only one in her family with N-Nurturing first. Everyone else was a B-Blueprint first code. They didn't understand why she kept giving her money away and letting her friends take advantage of her. She felt like she was broken, but no matter how hard she tried to change, she just couldn't do it.

After being trained on the B.A.N.K. system, the family realized no one was broken; each of them was just living up to his or her code. They gained clarity about the different codes and how to use them to their fullest potential and are now bully free. They have tamed the bully between their ears and realized why they did what they did. They also know how to change it.

B.A.N.K. gives you insight into how and why you make the decisions you do. Once you have awareness of yourself, you can make changes to what needs to change and keep the rest.

I have worked with so many families and individuals who have improved lives because of Bully Proofing You and

B.A.N.K. The pairing of these two programs has saved lives all over the world. I am so grateful to Cheri Tree for writing this book you're reading. She will help so many more people with the wisdom shared here. I will also use it as another resource for my clients to refer to. I like teaching people how to help themselves because the only person who is there for you 100 percent of the time is you.

Use what you have learned here to understand yourself and others better. It might just save the life of someone you love.

A NEW WAY TO MATCH

These stories testify that B.A.N.K. is more than just a personality type system. It's more than a business tool for closing a sale. It's a communication tool that helps us all to get along better with one another. It's been said that we only hurt the ones we love, but why that has to happen makes no more sense to me than why you need to collect nos to get a yes. When we learn each other's B.A.N.K. code, we can learn how to communicate with each other in ways that are win-wins for all of us. Imagine if you could search the next dating site based on a matching code, and not just "looks and personality." This could alter the entire dating process and even save tens of thousands of marriages. We may not even need so many marriage counselors or divorce attorneys. We just need to learn how to communicate with each other. I know I've said it before, but B.A.N.K. can change the world, starting in the office or in the home, one relationship at a time.

CHAPTER 19

THE GAME-CHANGER

"B.A.N.K. is a game-changer for every entrepreneur and sales professional. This system will strengthen your confidence, expand your selling skills, and dramatically increase your income."

— Les Brown

I call B.A.N.K. a game-changer because of the amazing impact it has had on my life and the lives of others. I'm not the only one who thinks so—but is that term really an accurate way to refer to B.A.N.K.?

The definition of a game-changer is an event, idea, or procedure that significantly shifts your current manner of doing or thinking about something.

Game-changers are rare; they don't come around that often. For something to be a game-changer, it totally has to transform what we do, say, or think.

@CheriTree #WhyTheyBuy

If B.A.N.K. really is a game-changer, then, you can't afford not to master it.

WHERE DO YOU NEED A GAME-CHANGER?

Let me ask you a question: Where do you need a game-changer? Do you need one in your business so you can close more sales and make more money? Do you like the idea of experiencing less rejection and more success?

Do you need a game-changer in your personal sales, or maybe your entire company, so you can clone your top producers, accelerate market growth, and crush your competition? Could this be the next big idea that you roll out at your company convention to push your company to the top of your industry and dramatically increase shareholder value?

Perhaps you need a game-changer in your marriage? Maybe the idea of opposites attracting was very alluring at first, but now you're experiencing opposites attacking instead? You may have heard that no amount of success in business can account for failure in the home. I wholeheartedly agree with that! I think that's where the saying came from, "Happy wife, happy life"!

Maybe you need a game-changer with your child, or children? You can be a total hero in your business world and be placed on every pedestal there is, but if you're a zero to your children, your life will feel empty and meaningless. Has it ever occurred to you that although your child may be born with your DNA, he or she may not be born with your B.A.N.K. code? Have you considered that how you parent one child may need to be totally different from how you parent another?

Are you open to the possibility that you can shift your family or business dynamic from dysfunctional to fully functional? Imagine how this could change the game for you!

B.A.N.K. is the single most impactful thing I have ever discovered. It has given me a skill set that not only closes more sales and makes me more money, but more importantly, it has given me the gift of the golden tongue.

For me, B.A.N.K. was that game-changer because it taught me something no one else could ever teach me—why they buy. Why they buy your products and services. Why they buy your ideas. Why they buy your vision. Why they buy into anything you do or say.

@CheriTree #WhyTheyBuy

I have reached a level of mastery and become so fluent in each code that I can speak the right language, at the right time, in any situation. I have become unconsciously competent, and the doors of opportunity that have opened and continue to open are mind-blowing!

B.A.N.K. IS A GAME-CHANGER FOR SALES—AND LIFE!

A few years ago, I had the chance to meet the amazing Les Brown, world-renowned speaker, coach, and best-selling author. He had been told about my B.A.N.K. system and wanted to know more about it. As I explained the secrets, the science, and the system to him, he told me it was a *game-changer*! He told me it was the most powerful system he'd ever seen for sales, anywhere in the world.

What originally started off as an experiment has turned into a movement. B.A.N.K. has spread virally into more than forty countries and counting, as a result of the powerful transformation it's making for our clients worldwide.

When you learn to crack the personality code—you're going to take it to the bank—your bank account! Think of the countless number of sales you have left on the table, simply because of your inability to deliver the right presentation to the right prospect. You spoke the wrong language—broke the vial of vinegar—and it cost you more than you could afford to lose.

If you own a sales organization, imagine the tens of thousands or hundreds of thousands or even millions of dollars being left on the table that are up for grabs by your competitor because your sales team continually fails to deliver the right presentation.

B.A.N.K. doesn't guarantee that you'll close every sale, but if it's closeable, your odds for closing that sale dramatically increase when you crack that personality code and take it to the *bank*. Understanding *why they buy* will give you a much greater advantage than simply trying to learn how to sell.

THANKS FOR LETTING ME SHARE THIS GAME-CHANGER WITH YOU

It's been an honor to write this book and share this incredible methodology with you. B.A.N.K. has changed my life! I can't imagine my life without it. I now see life in full color.

Not only has it changed my business and dramatically increased my income, but it has improved every single aspect of my personal relationships—and that part is priceless!

Today, I'm on a mission to change the world—beginning with your world! My mission is to create One World, One Language.

@CheriTree #WhyTheyBuy

B.A.N.K. is the language of people, and you can become multilingual when you study and apply its teachings. If you're able to benefit from it at just a fraction of what it has done for me—it will change your life and your business forever.

The next steps are completely up to you. If you're ready to take these principles and put them into action, you can experience extraordinary results. In the Bonus Section, I will share all the ways you can *take it to the bank*!

ARE YOU READY FOR A GAME-CHANGER?

- ❑ Are you ready to close more sales?
- ❑ Are you ready to make more money in less time?
- ❑ Are you ready to get more yeses and fewer nos?

- ❑ Are you ready to connect faster and easier with your prospects?
- ❑ Are you ready to deliver the right presentation 100 percent of the time?
- ❑ Are you ready to improve your communication skills?
- ❑ Are you ready to increase your sales up to 300 percent?

If the answer is Yes—then get ready to *take it to the bank*—before your competition does!

TAKING IT TO THE BANK – STEPHANIE B.

After years of performing on stages and building a successful voice coaching practice, I started to work with more entrepreneurs who wanted to build successful businesses of their own. I met Cheri Tree at the perfect time when I was about to rebrand and go in a new direction. My genius is knowing how to deliver a script with a powerful voice and stage presence. Cheri's genius is knowing how to write that script and change it on a moment's notice when needed. B.A.N.K. is one of the most powerful tools I now teach my clients, and it is a perfect complement to my methodology. Not only am I able to close more sales in my business, but my current clients are able to be more successful and I'm able to connect with them at a deeper level in our sessions.

Becoming a Certified B.A.N.K. Trainer was a natural progression given what I already do, and now I have been able to leverage my income and build a team that creates passive income in my business. As a result of learning B.A.N.K., I started consistently bringing in five figures for my business every month. After a couple of years of almost or barely breaking $100,000 per year, I brought in $50,000 of income in just the first quarter of 2017. My husband wants to retire in a couple of years, and for the first time ever, I see how we can create the lifestyle we desire while raising our five-year-old and being more fully present for each other as a family.

CHAPTER 20

INSIDE THE VAULT

> **"Every adversity, every failure, every heartache carries with it the seed of an equal or greater benefit."**
>
> **– Napoleon Hill**

This book has been filled with amazing success stories, including some of my own. For that, I am very grateful.

However, I want to share something with you that is very personal to me. Because you have honored me with your time by reading this book and learning from me, I want to honor you and share something that not a lot of people get to hear about. It's not about my massive success. It's about my massive failure, how I overcame that monumental adversity, and how you can too.

PEOPLE BEFORE PROFITS

Once I started using the B.A.N.K. methodology and experiencing such fantastic results, I couldn't keep it a secret any longer. I started training every sales team member who was part of my whole network. I wanted everyone to experience the benefits I was experiencing. If B.A.N.K. is really that big of a game-changer, the world deserved to know about it. However, my success was envied, and I reached a place where I was limited in my ability to train other people because of corporate politics.

I was faced with a major decision. Was I more about the money or integrity? As enticing as the fame and fortune was, I chose to stand up for what I believe in and put people before profits rather than vice-versa.

@CheriTree #WhyTheyBuy

It's sad to see how many people have it backwards—but I chose not to be one of them.

Instead, I resigned from the company I was working for on August 8, 2008. I then chose to start my own training company where I could share my game-changing methodology with the world. I didn't want to be limited or restricted in any way from sharing something that could change others' lives. I knew the pain of rejection and the agony of defeat intimately. I wanted to bring my vision and my mission to the world, and I wanted to make a difference, not just a dollar.

As a result, I walked away from nearly $2 million a year. My income went to zero overnight. With my entrepreneurial spirit, I expected I could climb back up that mountain.

THE HITCH IN THE PLAN

Unfortunately, I was immediately met with significant adversity. The company I resigned from sued me within ten days of my resignation, attempting to stop me from growing my own business. Unwilling to be bullied, I used every resource I had and fought it all the way through federal court. This was one of the worst battles of my life, and although I won the right to run my own business, I still lost everything.

Just like a perfect storm, 2008 also marked the collapse of a good portion of the entire American economy. I had about $8 million in real estate holdings at the time, and they all became worth nothing practically overnight. My cash flow situation went to a negative $60,000 per month, and in the blink of an eye, I was broke. Everything I'd been accumulating my entire life—my homes, my cars, my investments—disappeared before my eyes.

With all of my real estate foreclosed, I took all that I had left and loaded up five different storage units. Shortly thereafter, the storage unit company called me and said, "Cheri, your stuff is about to go to auction if we don't receive a payment." I was drowning in my own maytag!

Now because my whole financial life crumbled and I had no income or credit left, I was forced to the inevitable—filing Chapter 7 Bankruptcy. Again, in a moment, everything I had was gone. I had no credit. I had to give back my homes. I had to give back my cars. I only kept one car, but a tow truck company came out in the middle of the night trying to find it. I couldn't handle the stress of it anymore, so I just went and turned it in.

I literally had nothing left to my name.

CLIMBING BACK FROM THE BOTTOM

Being a resourceful entrepreneur, I decided rather than having my stuff go up for auction, I'd find a better, cheaper solution. Soon, I found a 1,600-square-foot storage unit in Newport Beach, California. It was a huge warehouse, with a roll-up door and enough room to store all of my belongings.

Coincidentally, at the back of the storage unit was a tiny little set of wooden steps that went up to a little loft, maybe around 150 or 200 square feet. In that moment, I suddenly had an idea, "What if I could actually move in here and make this my home." This would allow me to save all my money so I could invest back into building my training company.

Around the same time, I was asked by my good friend, Josh Higginbotham, to speak at his company's market launch event. It wasn't a paid speaking gig, but it gave my new little training company some exposure.

I needed any break I could get! After I trained the entire sales force about B.A.N.K., I received a standing ovation. Everyone wanted to buy the program. Unfortunately, I didn't have anything for sale. I hadn't developed it into a product at that point. It was more of a concept that I taught.

As I left the stage, a gentleman named McKinley Oswald chased after me to tell me, "Cheri, that's one of the best sales training programs I've ever seen. I want to help you turn it into a tangible product, as long as you're willing to pay for it."

Well, this was the break I was looking for, except that I didn't have the money to pay for it, and I didn't have the credit either. But I don't accept defeat, and failure is never an option. My mom always taught me, "Where there's a will, there's a way."

Now I knew it was the right thing for me to move into that storage unit.

LIFE IN A STORAGE UNIT

Life in a storage unit is an interesting story by itself. It was a huge warehouse in an industrial park, with florescent lights and no running water.

Luckily, I was a trained whitewater rafting guide and had taken a course on wilderness survival. Since failure was not an option, I went down to the local camp store and bought a five-gallon bucket called a Luggable Loo.

That five-gallon bucket came with a toilet seat, so I made that my bathroom for the next eighteen months. I bought a membership at the gym so I could shower. Some days I never made it to the gym, so I either didn't shower or just rinsed my head under the water spigot outside the building.

It was a crazy time, not that long ago. If we ever have the opportunity to meet, I can tell you some pretty funny stories...and some not-so-funny stories too.

Most importantly, what I want to share with you is that I'm not the type of person who stays down when life beats me up. We all have adversity. Some of us have more, and some have less. But we all have it. And that's how I know we can overcome it. I rebuilt my entire life from that place!

YOU'RE NEVER ALONE

Even when you feel alone, you're never alone. Luckily for me, I found one really good friend who loved me and believed in me. Her name is Jenny Luetkemeyer, and she's my best friend and co-founder of my company.

Since we were best friends and now business partners, I asked her whether she was willing to think outside the box and move into a little tiny box with me! I knew if we lived there together, it would feel more like camping, and I'd always loved to camp.

It was there in that little creepy storage unit that we took my decade of experience with B.A.N.K. and not only turned it into a revolutionary product but also built the foundation for a company that's now all over the world.

NO MATTER WHAT—WHATEVER IT TAKES

I'll never forget when I recorded the first soundtracks of B.A.N.K. so that I would have a set of CDs I could sell. It wasn't in a beautiful studio, soundproofed and equipped with boom microphones. Instead, I was in a storage unit where the windows were stuck permanently open for ventilation. Some of the first audio tracks of B.A.N.K. had barking dogs, helicopters, and police sirens in the background! I no longer sell CDs, but I bet those are collectible editions now. So if you have a set of those CDs, make sure you keep them—someday they could be worth some bank!

During the winter, we nearly froze to death, so we went to Costco and got a little portable heater. We'd huddle down by the bottom of it just to stay warm. I always prayed that it wouldn't catch on fire because that would have been the end—there aren't any escape routes in a storage unit because you're not supposed to live in one!

I could tell you story after story about the adversity I faced during that time.

The key for me was that failure was never an option.

@CheriTree #WhyTheyBuy

It wasn't an option in sports. It wasn't an option in the Girl Scouts or my candy business. It wasn't an option in my financial services business or my network marketing business. Now, it certainly wasn't an option in the storage unit while building my own business. The point is quitting was never an option. I was committed—no matter what—whatever it took!

WHAT DOESN'T KILL YOU MAKES YOU STRONGER

The best thing that ever happened to me was losing everything. Living in that storage unit for eighteen months erased my attachment to money. I had made millions and millions of dollars, but now I was no longer attached to money; instead, I grew my attachment to people and purpose. My heart expanded to three times its former size. I fell in love with people like never before. I fell in love with my purpose. I knew with total certainty that I am here to make a difference—far more than just to make a dollar.

B.A.N.K. has completely changed my heart from the inside out. It's not greed and success that's driving me—it's seeing the lives of every single person who gets in contact with B.A.N.K.'s incredible message and "changes in the blink of an eye."

Sure, on a surface level it's about sales, which is about making money, so the first impression B.A.N.K. gives is, "We can help salespeople make more money. We can help them close more sales."

But just stop and think what that really means for a human being—the ability to make more money. Think about the stress that comes into someone's life when he can't pay his bills. I've watched marriages destroyed right in front of my eyes because "money, money, money" is the constant topic of conversation and source of stress in a couple's life.

People want to quit their jobs. They want to be entrepreneurs, yet nine out of ten businesses fail within the first five years. They want to join network marketing and have a shot at creating some form of financial freedom, yet approximately 98 percent of network marketers make less than $500 a year. That is a crying shame, but now we have a system that can change those odds.

THE ODDS OF SUCCESS—AND FAILURE

We live in one of the greatest countries in the world, yet 95 percent of people in our own country at retirement age are flat busted broke. You want to know the statistics?

According to the Department of Health and Human Services, of all sixty-five-year-olds today in America:

- 54 percent are dependent upon the government, church, and family.
- 36 percent are still working. So much for retirement.
- 5 percent are dead. No thank you.
- 4 percent are financially independent. This used to sound exciting to me, and as a former financial advisor, it was my goal for my clients. Unfortunately, according to our government, this means that retirees are living on approximately \$3,000–\$4,000 a month. Not exactly the dream retirement you planned on, right?
- 1 percent are wealthy, with a net worth of \$5 million or more. That means 99 percent of our country is on track for financial disaster.

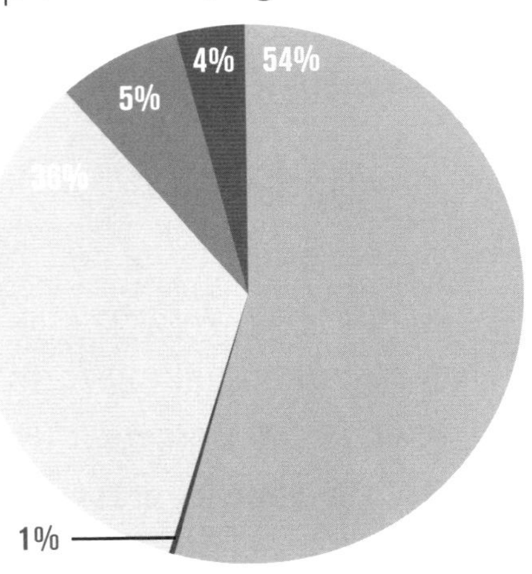

I've got to ask you right now, "How are you doing reaching that $5 million goal?" Only 1 percent can say, "I'm on track." If you're the lucky one in 100—congratulations! Unfortunately, most of the people you care about aren't that lucky.

MY WHY

Simon Sinek's book *Start With Why* really resonated with me. He taught that the reason you do something should drive the way you talk about it. My why for B.A.N.K. and my company BANKCODE is that I really want to make a difference for people. I would love to get access to every salesperson in the world, every business owner, every entrepreneur who has the courage to start something—to walk away from something, to do something, or to build something for his or her family and for him- or herself.

Self-esteem increases when you win, not when you lose. Unfortunately, the world is set up to make you fail. What if there's a company, a visionary, a missionary out there who cares about making a difference?

Our B.A.N.K. methodology will not only transform the face of your business but also revolutionize your relationships. It can completely rebuild your self-esteem and put you on track to living a life that most people only dream about.

I'm not just talking about the money. What if you had the secrets, the science, and the system not only to impact your finances but also to change the world? What if you could use this very science to build bridges, creating the most amazing relationships in the world? What if you had the key to understanding yourself, your spouse, your children, and everyone around you that you care about?

Our tagline as a company is, "One world, one language." We live on a planet with seven billion people. More than 6,500 different languages are spoken on Earth, but there's only one language that I believe unites the entire human race. That is B.A.N.K., the language of people.

B.A.N.K. is changing families, and families are changing communities. If we change enough communities, we can change humanity.

@CheriTree #WhyTheyBuy

ONE WORLD, ONE LANGUAGE

A few years ago, one of my B.A.N.K. clients came up to me and said, "Cheri, I think B.A.N.K. is going to win a Nobel Peace Prize one day."

The first time I heard that, I was shocked. I wasn't ready to accept that type of acknowledgment.

He said, "Think about it.... I come from Israel, a country torn by war. I have friends who are part of the United Nations.

The only reason countries go to war is because country leaders don't know how to communicate with each other."

Whether it's the wars of the world or the wars inside your business or your home, we have a solution that can bring peace to you and every community around the world: learning how to speak the language of people.

You want to know what Cheri Tree is really about? I'm about changing lives. I know that helping you make more money can change lives. Money can help you achieve your real dreams. Sure, people have told me, "Money doesn't buy you happiness." But when they say that, I usually reply, "Well, I recommend you try making at least a million dollars in one year and then reevaluate that saying!" That's another silly myth, right? Money definitely can buy you a lot of happiness, but money isn't everything.

You can do a lot of great things with money, but the best and most important thing is going out and making a difference in this world. Your life isn't just about you anymore; it becomes about the people whose lives you can touch and transform forever.

I believe in a concept I learned in the movie *Pay It Forward*. The movie proposed one question:

"Is it possible for one idea to change the world?"

@CheriTree #WhyTheyBuy

Then an assignment was given, "Think of an idea that can change the world and put it into motion."

My friend, thank you for allowing me to share my one idea… an idea called B.A.N.K., on track to change the world—starting with your world—and you can *take that to the bank*!

A FINAL NOTE

TAKING IT TO THE BANK

"Progress always involves risk. You can't steal second base and keep your foot on first."

– Frederick Wilcox

Congratulations on finishing *Why They Buy*! Statistically, the odds of people finishing a book are very low. Most people don't finish what they start. I'm flattered that you chose to finish this one. I truly believe it's a game-changer! But as my Harvard friends like to say, "So what, now what?"

Let's start with why.... Why did you read this book? Were you trying to crack the sales code and figure out why your customers buy? Were you looking for answers that could make you more money or save you more time? Were you looking to live the life you deserve?

My guess is your answer is yes to all of those questions! So what are you committed to doing so you can benefit from the secrets inside this book? What goals are you going to set? What actions are you going to take? What strategies will you implement?

I love the quote by Frederick Wilcox above. I was a softball player and loved to steal second base! Progress involves risk. Did you read this book just to say you read another book—or are you ready to harness the power of this book and start taking it to *your bank*?

Knowledge can only get you so far. A lot of very smart, but broke, people are out there. One of my clients told me he thought I used the color green for Knowledge because K's are often "green with envy." When I asked why he would say that, he explained that K's are often the smartest people in their departments, and sometimes in the entire company—but they're not the highest paid. Yikes! I can understand why that would create envy.

Yes, knowledge is power, but without action, you're still going to be stuck exactly where you were when you started reading this book. (Hopefully, you're at a beautiful tropical resort sipping on an umbrella drink—and if so—have one for me!). Applied knowledge is where the real power is.

So, it's time to get clear on what action you're going to take to make big things happen in your life. I challenge you to *take massive action*—now! The next step is to take what I've taught you and build your M.A.P.—Massive Action Plan. That is the only way you can monetize the million-dollar ideas I've shared with you.

Now I'd like to share my favorite formula for creating wealth. Ready?

MINDSET + SKILL SET = JET SET

@CheriTree #WhyTheyBuy

I know you have the right mindset because you bought this book and finished it. You're already ahead of the curve. Now all you need are the skill sets I taught you in these pages, and once you master them, you can live the jet set life.

I'll admit it—money can buy you happiness! Trust me. I've been rich and I've been broke—and broke sucks! You need a lot of money to achieve your goals and make your dreams come true. If you want to be wealthy, then you're going to need at least $5 million set aside. If you want to give a lot of money away, then you need to have even more. So, yes, money can buy you happiness. But, as I've said before, money isn't everything. That's the part you need to remember so you stay humble and willing to pay it forward, too.

Okay, so let's build your Millionaire M.A.P. What are the ten things you're committed to doing within the next ninety days as a result of reading this book? Put ink to paper by writing them down. (If you're a Blueprint, I know you probably don't want to write in this book, so you can type it up instead.)

1. ______________________________
____

2. ______________________________
____

3. ______________________________
____

4. ______________________________
____

5. ______________________________
____

6. ______________________________
____

7. ______________________________
____

8. ______________________________
____

9. ______________________________
____

10. ______________________________
____

One thing I recommend putting on your list of ten action items would be to go back and complete the exercises in this book. Don't just read this book, but study it. Journal notes from it. Practice its principles. I strongly recommend you reread the last section and find ways you can gain access to more information so you can achieve record sales and take it to the bank!

In this book, I taught you the secrets, the science, and the system you need to supercharge your sales in less than ninety seconds. I revealed four very powerful secrets that will help you get on the fast track to success and get unstuck from the sales maytag that may have been holding you back. Remember, sales is not a numbers game. It's a people game. Richard Branson says, "When it comes to business success, it's all about people, people, people."

I also revealed the science required for you to be more powerful in your communication. Using a combination of personality science, buyology, and sales linguistics, you can now find the missing link and be ready to deliver the right presentation, 100 percent of the time.

Next, I taught you the system for massive success. SYSTEM is an acronym. It stands for Save Your Self Time, Energy, and Money. The B.A.N.K. system is designed to increase your sales and communication skills up to 300 percent, and it has been field-tested for the past two decades, and even scientifically proven to predict buying behavior by San Francisco State University. When you carefully follow this system, step-by-step, you will unlock the power of your full potential in ways beyond your imagination.

Lastly, I shared with you the solution for putting all this valuable information into action. Without action, this is just simply a great idea. At the time of this writing, the world is just awakening to an understanding of B.A.N.K. on a grand scale. It has spread virally to more than forty countries because of the powerful results that thousands of clients are getting from around the world, but we still have far to go.

Now that you're reading this published book, it's only a matter of time before industry leaders get on board and start to implement these proven strategies into their businesses. Don't get left in the dust by your competition. If you wake up every day with the hungry attitude to fight for your dreams, then I choose to fight for you too. You have in your hands one of the most powerful concepts to hit modern day businesses. Use it. Learn it. Bank on it!

If you apply the wisdom, knowledge, experience, skills, strategies, and techniques offered in this book to your life and your business, you will achieve record sales and real wealth like the world's top achievers. You are moments away from starting to reach your goals and live your dreams. All you need to do is simply apply what you've learned right now!

Because you've read my book, I encourage you to contact me and share with me how it has impacted your business, your sales, your income, and your life.

I want you to be my next big success story! Share your success stories with me.

I want to hear how you used your B.A.N.K. value cards on an appointment where you closed the sale because you knew the person's code, just like Darren Goonawardana, who closed a $250,000 deal using the cards.

Or how you used your B.A.N.K. PASS link to code your leads, and then marketed to them differently, like Esther Wildenberg did and closed €35,000 in more revenue from one BANKIFIED email campaign.

Or I'd love to hear from you that you subscribed to our live or virtual courses and got to practice using B.A.N.K. with one of our certified and licensed trainers, like Stephanie Bonte-Lebair, who had a series of consecutive yeses and closed 100 percent of all her sales for an entire month! This type of extraordinary success is possible for you.

Perhaps you want to share a more personal story with me about how B.A.N.K. has impacted your marriage, like it did for Azita Demalignon, or how it helped your parenting, like it did for Anna Parker, or maybe it helped to reduce bullying in schools, like the story I got from Jeannie Cisco-Meth.

Whatever your success story, I'd love to hear it straight from you. Send me an email at whytheybuy@bankcode.com. I read each email because your stories fuel my passion to keep sharing this system with the world. If you want to join me on social media, I'd love to connect! You can find all my social media links on my personal website, cheritree.com.

If you want to book me to speak at your conference, I can promise you an experience like none other. You may as well take your shoes off now—because I'm about to blow your socks off! You can find more info about my speaking engagements in the back of this book, or on my website: cheritree.com.

Thank you for the opportunity to share my teachings with you! I wish you all the success and happiness in the world, and I can promise you that when you apply the principles of the B.A.N.K. methodology to your life, you will forever see a life in full color.

Good luck, my friend! Great success and prosperity await you! I look forward to hearing from you or meeting you at an upcoming event.

Take it to the bank!

GETTING STARTED

UNLOCK YOUR ACCESS

Over the preceding four sections, I've given you an insider look at the ins and outs of B.A.N.K., shared stories about B.A.N.K.'s game-changing power from my own life and from the lives of members throughout the B.A.N.K. community, and given you the full foundation you need to start changing your life through B.A.N.K.

At this point, you're probably eager to put these tools and systems to work in your business. To help you get the fastest results in the shortest amount of time, I'm offering three ways to access our solutions and help you fully implement B.A.N.K. into your business and life:

1. **Self-Implementation:** Gain access to our powerful training, tools, and technology needed to supercharge your business and fast track your success with your own initiative.

2. **Professional Implementation:** Engage a professional certified and licensed B.A.N.K. trainer to consult with you and lead you through the B.A.N.K. implementation process, customized to your specific business.
3. **Private Implementation:** Work directly with me and my top corporate team to develop a full B.A.N.K. implementation strategy customized for your global business needs.

You can find out more about these three approaches, crack your code, subscribe to our blog, find out how to become a professional certified trainer or authorized reseller, and schedule private consulting or speaking engagements at bankcode.com.

If you have any other questions or want any additional help, call (702) 342-0742 or email whytheybuy@bankcode.com.

YOUR ACCESS CODE

Use this special Access Code to unlock your access to special offers, tools, reports, and more at bankcode.com.

mybankcode.com/dianadeene

Diana Deene
310.210.1646

ACKNOWLEDGMENTS

I want to acknowledge numerous special people who have played amazing roles in my life as coaches and mentors: Robert Kiyosaki, Tony Robbins, Les Brown, John Maxwell, Brian Tracy, Stephen Covey, Richard and Veronica Tan, Sandra Yancey, Hans Keirstead, and the cast on *Shark Tank*. I have learned so much from you in business and in life. Thank you.

In addition, I want to acknowledge our talented affiliates, consultants, and certified and licensed trainers who have pledged a part of their lives to teaching this powerful message to the world. You mean the world to me and I'm so thankful that your hearts and minds have aligned with my vision to change the world and create One World, One Language.

I also want to acknowledge and thank my internal team members and strategic consultants who are committed to our vision and push the boundaries every day to play at a Level 10. Specifically, Esther Wildenberg, Jenny Luetkemeyer, Tom Tree, Tami Russaz, Anna Parker, Jason Gust, Dan Scott, Lauren Scott, Kaitlin Goodrich, Svetlana Hodoba, Gagan Sarkaria, John Kurth, Brad Lea, Josh Higginbotham,

Cory Jim, and Yancey Unequivocally. I am forever grateful for your hard work and contribution toward our mission.

I finally want to acknowledge those who really helped me with my book, starting with my book coach, Patrick Snow. Thank you for coaching me, guiding me, and pushing me to put my very best into writing this book. Your mentorship has been priceless and I'm in deep gratitude to you for holding me accountable and helping me get this work done so that the world could benefit from it as soon as possible. I would also like to thank Kaitlin Goodrich for your help with the copywriting so that my book made sense! A special thanks to Svetlana Hodoba for the cover design and every piece of our iconic brand, Fusion Creative Works for the layout, and Tyler Tichelaar for his amazing editing skills. You all did a fantastic job, and you made me proud to share this book with the world!

"People buy into the leader before they buy into the vision."

— John Maxwell, American Author, Speaker, and Pastor

ENTREPRENEUR | SPEAKER | TRAINER | AUTHOR

ABOUT CHERI TREE

@cheritree #WhyTheyBuy

Cheri Tree is a successful entrepreneur, professional keynote speaker, world-renowned sales trainer, best-selling author, and executive business coach. She is the founder and CEO of BANKCODE, with clients in more than 40 countries worldwide. Cheri has spoken to hundreds of thousands of entrepreneurs and sales professionals globally and been featured in numerous international publications, sharing the stage with icons such as Tony Robbins, Robert Kiyosaki, Suze Orman, and Sir Richard Branson.

"The ability to sell is the number one skill in business... You've got to sell! Cheri Tree will teach you how to sell."

– Robert Kiyosaki

Cheri has also lectured at Harvard University and the University of California at Berkeley and is considered the number one personality-based sales trainer in the world. Her expertise earned her the American Riviera Woman Entrepreneur of the Year Award, and she's been nominated for the Women in Business award and Innovator of the Year award by the *Orange County Business Journal*. In order to teach B.A.N.K. to anyone who wants to learn, Cheri wrote her ground-breaking book *Why They Buy*. When not traveling the world to share B.A.N.K., Cheri lives with her beautiful family in Laguna Beach, California.

BOOK CHERI TREE TO SPEAK TO YOUR ORGANIZATION

Cheri Tree has gained a reputation as one of the most powerful keynote speakers in the business world, due to her dynamic approach to personality-based sales training. When Cheri teaches B.A.N.K., she doesn't just give your organization another "trick" to close a sale better that will be forgotten soon after she leaves. Cheri instead instills the fundamentals of how to communicate more effectively both on sales calls and in everyday interpersonal interactions.

A dynamic and engaging speaker, Cheri has appeared on hundreds of stages in front of millions of people around the world, teaching the secrets of success in sales to entrepreneurs, Fortune 500 companies, and even students at top universities like Harvard University. In fact, Cheri has been featured at conferences in Asia, Africa, Europe, and North America. She has even shared the stage with other celebrity speakers.

Few speakers can entertain and inform throughout an entire keynote speech. Cheri is the rare exception, which makes her one of the most in-demand speakers in her field. Beyond just entertaining, Cheri's keynotes, speeches, and interactive workshops deliver real results. Not all speakers are equally skilled at training smaller groups or even effectively educating the audience on the topics at hand. Cheri Tree is. She knows how to balance interactive entertainment with in-depth learning experiences, so everyone comes away with the vital knowledge needed to increase sales dramatically.

Book Cheri today as a keynote speaker for your next conference, in-house training day, keynote talk, or event. Whether you are looking for a featured speaker for a ninety-minute keynote or an experienced trainer to deliver a full-day workshop, Cheri Tree is uniquely qualified to provide a fun, educational presentation that your whole organization will love.

Book Cheri Tree To Speak At Your Next Event Or Get More Information About Her Keynotes Now

whytheybuy@bankcode.com | (702) 342-0742

To learn more about Cheri's approach and topics of expertise, watch clips of her past speeches, or download her media kit, visit cheritree.com.